Ossie Dale

Above: Rummy parades in the 1980's before the running of the great Liverpool race, which he did so much to save. A snapshot I took.

Right: After a hard day's ploughing I return, in 1956, with my two faithful Shires, who were waiting for me when I first went to work at Aintree in 1953.

Ossie Dale's Grand National Scrapbook

by Reg Green

Foreword by Lord Oaksey

Marlborough/Punchestown

MARLBOROUGH BOOKS
6 Milton Road, Swindon, SN1 5JG
c/o 9 Queen Street, Melbourne 3000, Victoria,

PUNCHESTOWN BOOKS
Ormond Court, 11 Lower Ormond Quay, Dublin 1

First Published 1992

Authors' Thanks
We would like to thank everyone who has allowed us to reproduce photographs both professional (especially Kris Photography and Colin Turner) and amateur.

Design, Typesetting and Artwork
Typographical Services, High Wycombe, Bucks, England

Printed by Regent Publishing Services Limited
Hong Kong

ISBN 1-873919-04-2 Marlborough
ISBN 1-873920-02-4 Punchestown

Foreword

I am delighted to hear that Ossie Dale's story is at last being told. As long as I can remember Ossie has played a vital part in the running of Aintree and the Grand National. Like his great friend and colleague, the late John Hughes, he never lost faith in either the place or the race. Without these two the National might never have reached its present position of comparative security.

Ossie was looking after the Aintree stables and working on the course with his beloved Shire horses before I had my first ride there - on Minimax - a distant second in the 1956 Foxhunters. He was still going strong when I rather belatedly hung up my boots in 1975.

We did have the occasional difference of opinion and I was once bold enough to suggest that Ossie might have built the third fence an inch or so too high. It is, you'll remember, an open ditch and I was not the only participant that year who thought it resembled the Grand Canyon. Needless to say Ossie and his trusty measuring stick soon put us straight!

All I want to do now - and everyone who has ridden at Aintree in the past forty years will want to do the same - is to wish Ossie a long happy retirement with a place of honour from which to watch many more Grand Nationals. His book gives a real insight into how Aintree works. I hope it sells and sells.

Pre-Aintree Days

My father's family came from Brassington in Derbyshire, although he moved to Liverpool to work and I was born there. As a child I used to go back to stay with Aunts and Uncles in Brassington where I spent much time in the local blacksmiths and soon formed a deep love of all horses, especially the Shires - the 'gentle giants'.

On leaving school I went to work on a farm at Lydiate, three or four miles from Aintree, where I progressed to a horse ploughman.

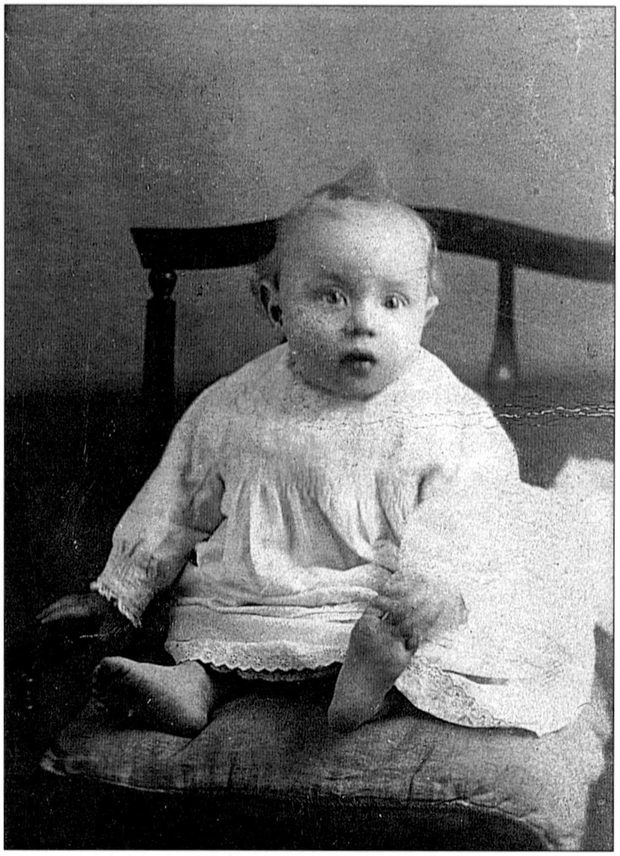

A picture of me during the First World War

Father (extreme right) and his brothers and sisters. Their total age was 481 years.

Bolton Abbey in August 1939 with Joan, Mother and her dog Jack.

Myself in Scout Uniform in 1938.

Joan and myself got married at Walton Church on Valentines Day 1942.

Happy days with Prince (left) and Dolly (right). This picture was taken in 1957.

The 1950's

I encountered for the first time the notorious Mrs. Topham while engaged one day in late October, 1953, scything long grass beneath the running rails between Valentines Brook and the Anchor Crossing. A most enlightening meeting it certainly way. I had started work the previous month as a horse ploughman on her farm.

Intent as I was on the task in hand, and with thoughts drifting to the exciting prospect of thoroughbreds racing across this land in a little over a week's time, a precise and well modulated voice brought my daydreams to an abrupt halt.

"Good afternoon, you must be Dale." Her words startled me to attention, and turning I was confronted by the commanding figure of Mirabel Dorothy Topham. "I hope you're happy here, the course is looking splendid and you're doing an excellent job with that scythe."

In that first ten minute conversation, I discovered just what an unfair image the newspapers can depict of a person. For not only was Mrs. Topham a thoroughly nice lady, she cared deeply for her employees and their families, just as she so obviously did about Aintree and the race which was its showpiece. Upon discovering that I had been associated with horses for nearly all my working life, Mrs. Topham informed me that for all future race meetings I would be in charge of the stables. This came as a most unexpected, though pleasing, addition to my duties; so much so, that it never even occurred to me to enquire if there would be any increase to my wages of four pounds, five shillings per week.

It was in this new role that I enthusiastically entered the mysterious yet essential backroom of horseracing, a quiet but most definite feeling of pride entering my mind with the knowledge that I was being entrusted with the care of extremely valuable race-horses.

That first walk around the extensive stabling complex at Aintree was to me like taking a step back in time, strolling through long past avenues of sporting history. Many of those antiquated stables bore mute testimony to by-gone glories, the names of such as Grudon, Reynoldstown, Golden Miller and Battleship having been reverently and affectionately painted on the box doors. Even if old fashioned, and in some cases a little the worse for wear, each box contained everything needed to provide warmth and comfort for its equine occupant.

Amazingly, I learned, there were five major stable yards on the racecourse and I at once made my headquarters at what is possibly the most easily identifiable, Paddock Yard. With accommodation for fifty horses, it is situated to the rear right of the Grandstands, well within sight of the National start, and the first box on the left just inside the gate became my office. New Yard provided the largest stabling facility, with one hundred and thirty-seven stalls, then Melling Road Yard with fifty-five boxes. Named after our local Earls, the Sefton and Derby Yards were capable of housing twenty and twelve

THE WORST VIEW IN EUROPE

"Oh Murther! The dhrink died out of me and the wrong side of Bechers"

I have a lovely large collection of Grand National material; above a Christmas card from perhaps the most famous racing print in the world "The Worst View in Europe" by Snaffles. It is of a jockey riding into Bechers in the 1901 race, won by Grudon. The caption is:-
"Oh Murther! The dhrink died out of me and the wrong side of Bechers"..

Another Christmas card showing a Grand National scene. This time of the 1912 Grand National won by Jerry M, ridden by Lester Piggot's grandfather, Ernie. The artist here is Alfred Bright whose son still attends the race regularly.

horses respectively, the latter facility being the location in which any Royal competitors were stabled.

Amid excited hustle and bustle, the final touches for my first 'real meeting' were faithfully applied. Aintree emerged from its summer break looking resplendent and on Wednesday 4th November 1953 I came face to face with my first real National hero. The great 'Liverpool horse' Freebooter was led to Bobbie Renton's box in New Yard, looking every inch the champion he undoubtedly was. Although now twelve years old, having proved himself the finest jumper of the big Liverpool fences since the War, he had returned to the course he knew so well for what was to be his final race. It was a mixed meeting, like that in the Spring, chases, hurdles and flat races.

It was on the level that the consistent Durante won the first of what was to be an outstanding hat-trick in the Liverpool Autumn Cup. Then, as now, though my main interest in the sport concerned racing over the sticks and for like minded people, we were as usual treated to some rare delights. Little Yid, who had started favourite for the National barely seven months earlier, got the Renton stable off to the best possible of starts on the first day with a clear cut victory in the Molyneaux Steeplechase, providing jockey George Slack with his first taste of success over the National fences. Twenty-four hours later that rider took the leg-up on the mighty Freebooter in the two mile five furlong Becher Chase and despite, with his top weight of twelve stone seven pounds conceding two stone to each of his ten rivals, gave one of the most perfect displays of fencing ever seen at Liverpool. Toying with the opposition for the entire journey, the former Grand National winner raced home three lengths clear to rapturous applause. In the opening race of the last day of that meeting, the incomparable Bryan Marshall produced one of his famous nail-biting finishes in the Prospect Hurdle, getting up on the line with the Fred Rimell trained Solar City to win by a neck from Mr. Eric Cousins on Greystown. Long considered a good guide to future Grand National hopefuls, the Grand Sefton Chase again attracted a field of useful seasoned jumpers and it was the turn of the Irish with the Pat Taaffe ridden Coneyburrow finishing the stronger from the popular locally owned Irish Lizard.

Less than a month later I was back in the stables again for the inaugural meeting over the Mildmay Course. Laid out and developed on the Stands side of the racecourse on the suggestion of the late Lord Mildmay, the new track was intended as an introduction for young horses before having to face the severity of the National fences proper. It had been intended to race over this course in the December of 1952 but Aintree had been in the grip of frost, so I count myself fortunate that this milestone in history was delayed until I was present. The opening ceremony was performed by Lord Mildmay's sister, Mrs. Mildmay-White, and although the races at the two-day fixture attracted only small fields, they were competitive affairs with Bryan Marshall proving his mastery by riding the first three winners.

With the New Year came the anxious task of preparing Aintree for its biggest day, the 1954 Grand National. Every member of the staff pulled out all the stops in their efforts to surpass previous years' achievements. Gorse and spruce was cut and collected from far and wide, a number of fences were completely rebuilt. It was the policy to do so on a rota basis each year in those days and repairs were carried out to the numerous stands and buildings. All this, together with painting of rails, barns and stables, was done by the permanent staff of Tophams and it was only in the last few weeks before the big event that temporary employees were engaged. Everything had to be ready to the satisfaction of Mrs. Topham at least a fortnight before National day, for the visit of racecourse inspector Major Gilbert Cotton, and of course for the examination by the general public on Jump Sunday. For the first time, during those hectic weeks, I came to realise just how much organisation, energy and effort went into the preparation of Aintree for the big one and, imbued with the enthusiasm which became an essential part of the place, I was determined that the stables would not be lacking in their contribution to the proceedings.

Unlike the first Mildmay meeting four months earlier, there was a frightening abundance of runners for my baptism of fire at the Spring fixture, with no less than one hundred and nineteen horses due to compete in the seven National Hunt races alone, quite apart from all those arriving for the flat events. Every horse entering the stable complex had to be entered in the stable register, together with the name of its trainer. Only when this formality was completed could keys to the boxes be issued and it was at this time that I came to understand that many racehorse trainers are quite superstitious, requesting the same stalls they have occupied in past visits. It was also on this occasion that I began the habit of choosing to sleep at the stables during National week. The loft above my little office in Paddock Yard was turned into a makeshift bedroom and I felt comfortable in the knowledge that I was on hand should an emergency occur.

Little Yid came good again for George Slack and Bobbie Renton on the opening day, winning a close fought finish to the Topham Trophy Chase. On the eve of the big race Bryan Marshall gave favourite backers palpitations when piloting Mr. Joe Griffin's Stroller to a mere head victory in the Coronation Hurdle. On the big day itself, Bryan carried on exactly where he left off, winning the hotly contested Liverpool Hurdle with Galatian by three-quarters of a length, and an hour and a half later, rode the race of his life on Royal Tan to just resist the late challenge of Tudor Line by a neck in the National. It must surely be something of a record for a jockey to partner the winners of three major Aintree races including the Grand National by an accumulated successful margin of barely one length within twenty-four hours.

There was, tragically, a very sad side to that year's big race, and one which affected me so deeply that I came very close to handing in my notice. Four horses lost their lives in the event forcing me, in the worst possible way, to face the harsh realities of steeplechasing. Thankfully it was Mrs. Topham herself who provided the understanding and reassurance to view such sorrow and sense of loss in a sympathetic yet logical way. Meeting me on the Monday after the race, she immediately recognised my disquiet, and having listened to my plaintive sentiments at the loss of such beautiful and noble creatures, once again surprised me with her genuine concern and sincerity.

"I know exactly how you feel, Dale." She spoke gently, yet with undeniable conviction. "You have seen for the first time at close range, what I have faced too often many times through the years. Sadly

Left: The last in 1935, Thomond II leads the winner Reynoldstown who was ridden by his trainer/owner's son, Frank Furlong. Next year Reynoldstown won again ridden by Fulke Walwyn who trained many winners at Aintree in my day, including the 1964 winner of the great race Team Spirit.

Right: Bechers, second time round, in 1931, when the race was won by Grakle. The crowd of people to the right of the fence, in the middle distance, are getting a free view from the footpath. This is from where, in 1929, I saw my first National.

Right: Bechers, first time round, 1938. The winner this year was the American horse, Battleship, ridden by Bruce Hobbs who beat Dan Moore on Royal Danieli by a head.

Left: Bechers, first time round, in the 1934 race, the year Dorothy Paget's Golden Miller won. He had won his third Cheltenham Gold Cup a few days before.

it never becomes easier; but you know, accidents occur even away from the hurly-burly of the racecourse. On the gallops, in transit to various meetings and even when out running free in a pasture. There is nothing more devastating than the sight of an injured animal and nobody feels greater grief at the loss of a horse than those most closely connected with it. You know, sometimes good can come from a tragedy such as this and who knows what may happen in the years ahead?"

I firmly believe that even then Mrs. Topham was contemplating some alteration to the racecourse or the fences.

Christmas came early in 1954, with the December meeting over the new Mildmay course being termed the Yuletide meeting, the paddock and stands decorated in festive bunting and tinsel and Mrs. Topham's nephew, Jim Bidwell-Topham dressed as Father Christmas for his job of handing out presents from a giant Christmas tree. That highly talented Irish jockey Tim Molony rode four of the six winners on the Wednesday.

It was a cold, depressing winter, snow and frost interfering with many race fixtures that the Cheltenham Festival had to be reduced to two days. With the thaw came persistent rain, and though we knew the heavy state of the ground was going to make jumping those big fences even more demanding than usual, none of us guessed that the National would be in danger of being abandoned. But it most certainly was, as we were horrified to discover on the morning of the race when the course was inspected again and again by the Stewards. It was only at noon that the go-ahead was given, and then with the proviso that the water jump be omitted in consideration of the waterlogged state of the ground in that area. Among the thirty runners was the Royal challenger M'As-Tu-Vu, and two previous winners of the race, Royal Tan and Early Mist. From the second last fence the race became a procession, Pat Taaffe bringing Quare Times home from the tiring Tudor Line and Carey's Cottage to win as he liked by twelve lengths. Yet another record in the most famous of all races, for the victory provided Irish trainer Vincent O'Brien with his third successive victory in the event.

It was back to the land and ploughing again for me as usual, once the vacated stables had been cleaned out, although I now found my work area in the inside of the racecourse had been slightly reduced by the recent construction of the motor race track. After various autosport notables had driven round the circuit, it was widely acclaimed as the finest of its kind in the whole of Europe. In mid-July, 1955 it was truly put to the test by most of the top international drivers when Aintree staged the British Grand Prix. Although the first three cars to reach the chequered flag were all Mercedes-Benz vehicles, the winning driver was none other than Stirling Moss, an Englishman through and through.

There can be little doubt that to even those without any interest in racing, the 1956 Grand National was by far the most dramatic and mystifying in the long history of the event. As the big day approached, there existed hopeful speculation that Her Majesty, Queen Elizabeth The Queen Mother, would at last be rewarded for her outstanding contribution to steeplechasing by winning the National. Her two representatives, Devon Loch and M'As-Tu-Vu, had

Bechers second time in the 1956 Grand National. Nearest to the camera taking the fence in great style is Dick Francis in HM The Queen Mother's colours on Devon Loch. They seemed certain winners approaching the post, but 50 yards from the line Devon Loch collapsed in one of the great mysteries of the Grand National and ESB won.
Insert: Barbara and Geoffrey in Padock Yard with ESB the next day.

The Christmas Party in 1956, my children Barbara and Geoffrey are far right. These parties were a regular treat provided by Mrs Topham for the children of the staff.

A staff day out. When the Tophams ran Aintree there were always children's parties, Christmas parties, staff outings and a 'ham supper' in the summer.

The Dale Family are all great cyclists. When my son Geoffrey was young we used to go on a week's cycling holiday every summer, often to Scotland.

Above: Grandson Jimmy's first bike ride in the early 1960s.

Right: Geoffrey without another living soul except me in sight, high in the Scottish Mountains in the early 1950s.

March 1983, Jimmy Stevenson and I training during our lunch hour for the sponsored bike ride around Aintree in aid of the Grand National Appeal. Most of our practice runs were in beautiful weather however the day we performed in earnest must have been the worst day of the Spring.

both come through a well planned preparation by trainer Peter Cazalet with encouraging performances.

As if as a prelude to that great longed for Royal occasion, the jumping sport on the first two days was of sufficiently high standard to whet the appetite of the most voracious connoisseur. The former triple Champion Hurdle winner Sir Ken ran out an easy winner in the Mildmay Chase to prove he was just as fluent over fences as hurdles. For the riders, there were successes for Fred Winter, Johnny Gilbert and Tim Molony and in the Foxhunters' an up and coming amateur by the name of The Honourable John Lawrence came second with Minimax in his first acquaintance with the unusual National fences. It was a name which was to become familiar to all associated with racing, his talent in the saddle being equalled by spirited use of the written word as one of our foremost racing journalists.

The 1956 Grand National without doubt produced the most sensational finish to any horserace in the history of the sport and with it, a mystery which is as unfathomable today as it was on that sad March afternoon so long ago.

Of the twenty-nine runners which set out, only eight had dropped from the contest by the time they reached the halfway stage, and to the delight of everybody Devon Loch was well in contention as Armorial III continued making the running back out onto the final circuit. When the second favourite, Sundew, came down at Bechers the race was really on in earnest, with Devon Loch and E.S.B. in hot pursuit of the leader and Eagle Lodge and the Northumberland trained mare Gentle Moya both close up. As foot perfect at the last fence as he had been throughout, the Royal champion powered his way into a decisive lead well before reaching the elbow, the deafening roars from the packed stands and enclosures endorsing not just his superiority but also the tremendous affection felt for his owner. Countless times since that fateful day, that final half-furlong gallop from joy to utter despair, has been shown on television with the approach of the latest National, but only those at Aintree when Devon Loch seemingly reached for an invisible obstacle, to lose his moment of glory spreadeagled on the turf within thirty yards of the post, can fully appreciate the true drama of that occasion and the instant eerie silence which followed.

Devon Loch's owner proved that day, if proof were ever needed, that she was every inch a Queen, hiding her intense disappointment as she congratulated the winning connections of E.S.B. and then commiserated with the disconsolate Dick Francis.

As a result of falling attendances, Mrs. Topham decided that the 1957 Grand National would be run on a Friday, a return to pre-war tradition. As an experiment it proved a total failure, and equally depressing was the weather, with constant rain making the occasion distinctly unpleasant for all concerned. The race itself though, brought a well deserved triumph for Fred Winter aboard the giant, free-running chestnut Sundew. Quite apart from providing the incomparable Fred Winter with his first success in the race, that 1957 National produced two names which for many years ahead were to be on countless lips each spring. A seven year old Scottish trained horse called Wyndburgh gave a faultless display on jumping to get within eight lengths of the winner at the line and just six lengths further in

Motor Racing started soon after I arrived at Aintree, the cars went the opposite way to the horses.
I took this picture in the summer of 1957.

Dick Farrington has a long trek with a heavy load.

The lorry we used to collect spruce in the early 1950s. It was back breaking work carrying and loading the spruce.

The last fence in 1958, Mr. What trained in Ireland by old Tom Taaffe and ridden by A. Freeman jumps the last to win. The fences were very much more upright in those days before their modification in the early 1960s.

arrears came the game and lovely mare owned and trained by Edward Courage, Tiberetta.

Wyndburgh quickly established himself as a genuine Liverpool horse when returning to Aintree that autumn, running out a convincing winner of the Grand Sefton and thereupon being earmarked for the 1958 National. The Scottish champion wound up 6/1 favourite on the day from the previous year's market leader Goosander at 100/7, but there was a formidable contingent from Ireland this time, led by the Duchess of Westminster's, Pat Taafe ridden Sentina. Almost ignored in the betting of those from across the Irish Sea was the tiny eight year old Mr. What, considered by many to be little more than a novice despite being trained by Tom Taaffe, father of the enormously talented jockeys Pat and Toss Taaffe. With both his sons booked for other horses, the mount on Mr. What went to the former Royal jockey Arthur Freeman who passed the clerk of the scales with six pounds overweight. It made not the slightest difference to the result though, Mr. What completely spreadeagling his field to win by no less than thirty lengths, after giving his connections a frightening moment at the last fence by pecking badly on landing. Tiberetta was second, in front of Green Drill and Wyndburgh.

Once again Tiberetta had shown just how well she took to the supreme demands of Aintree, a place where it seemed impossible for her to run a bad race. In the autumn of her brave second to Mr. What, the Banbury trained mare gave a faultless jumping performance to carry off the Grand Sefton Chase by three lengths from Green Drill.

The 1959 Grand National resulted in one of the most exciting duels of jockeyship ever seen at that historic venue. Both Tim Brookshaw and Michael Scudamore were farmer's sons, who progressed from point-to-points and the hunting field through undistinguished amateur status to the everyday cut and thrust of the top paid ranks of jockeys.

Surprise Packet made all the early running, providing Gerry Scott with a thrilling first ride in the race, but was starting to tire when falling at the second Bechers where Oxo with Michael Scudamore up and Wyndburgh with Tim Brookshaw up moved into contention. Having lost an iron through a stirrup leather breaking, Tim Brookshaw quickly and naturally kicked the other foot free and rode without stirrups for the remainder of the trip. After another pile-up at the Canal Turn, only six were left standing going into Valentines, with Oxo and Wyndburgh jumping perfectly well in front. Approaching the final fence, Oxo held a distinct advantage over Wyndburgh, with the favourite coming with a late flourish, but the leader stood too far off the fence and it was only the fine jockeyship of Michael Scudamore which prevented a last minute upset. Recovering well, the former point-to-pointer still held a commanding lead at the elbow and then Brookshaw came with an heroic challenge, cutting down the margin between Wyndburgh and Oxo stride by stride. It was a finish fit to bring a glow to anybody's tired heart, two great jockeys with their brave mounts conjuring up unbelievable reserves of energy in one last desperate quest for eternal glory. At the post it was Oxo by a length and a half, yet on that final National day of the 'fifties', both Scudamore and the unlucky Brookshaw shared the spoils of admiration and respect of all those privileged enough to witness their sporting brilliance. The only other two to complete the course were Mr. What and the ever faithful Tiberetta.

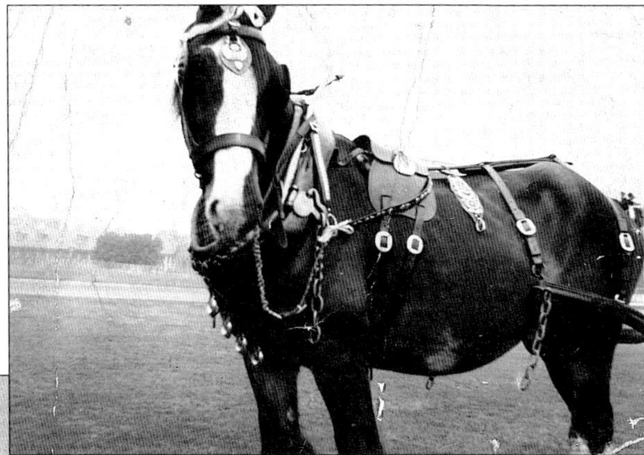

Ploughing with Prince and Dolly in the Autumn of 1959. Prince ready to go into a cart rather than ploughing; you will notice the different harness.

1960, the first year the Grand National was televised. The leaders over Bechers, second time round, Tea Fiend who finished fourth; Badanloch, ridden by Stan Mellor who finished second; the winner, Merryman II, ridden by Gerry Scott.
Merryman II was trained by Captain Neville Crump, who had won the race before with Teal in 1952 and Sheila's Cottage in 1948.

The 1960s

For those critics who claimed the falling attendances at Aintree in the late fifties were an indication that the Grand National was losing its appeal, the news that the race would be televised by the British Broadcasting Corporation in 1960 must have come as something of a shock.

Long considered as the obvious sporting subject for small screen viewers, many years of intense and sometimes frustrating discussion between the concerned parties at long last resulted in the exciting prospect that in future years the event would command a far greater audience than ever before.

For us backroom boys at Aintree, little changed except that our hectic final weeks before the big race were now conducted amid a seeming chaotic intrusion of cable layers, camera operators and production personnel. With such famous names as Peter O'Sullevan, Peter Dimmock and that great Irish commentator Michael O'Hehir walking the course for days before the race our normal everyday work suffered constant distractions. But there could be no question that the whole enterprise was an overwhelming success.

The result too was precisely just what the public most wanted, with the favourite Merryman II coming home a fifteen length winner from Lord Leverhulme's Badanloch in the smallest field since 1920. The winner provided trainer Neville Crump with his third victory in the race and there was a strange coincidence in that Merryman II became the first clear favourite to succeed in the race since Sprig in 1927, on a day when the B.B.C. were also involved in the proceedings, on that occasion relaying the first radio broadcast of the event.

The racecourse executive at last succumbed to the fierce criticism which for years had been directed against the National and those so famous 'walls' of spruce and gorse were modified in time for the 1961 race. By sloping the tops of the obstacles, and adding a fender with guard rail in front of the fences, it was felt competing horses would have a much fairer chance of both judging their line of approach together with an easier trajectory in jumping.

With joint sponsors, Messrs. Schweppes and the Irish Hospital Sweepstakes together adding £10,000 to Topham's usual £7,000, the first prize of £18,270 was a record for the race which this year was the focus of even greater attention than normal due to the international flavour of the contestants. Three Soviet horses, Epigraf II, Reljef and Grifel arrived at Haydock Park a number of weeks early to complete their preparation. As a three-time winner of Czechoslovakia's notoriously hazardous Velka Pardubice Steeplechase, Epigraf II was considered the pick of the trio. He went wrong, however, just days before the race, leaving the other two and French challenger Imposant as mainland Europe's challenge against thirty-two opponents.

Having kept his form well since last year's victory, Merryman II was always prominent in the antepost

A MERRY CHRISTMAS

1966

THIS IS THE CENTENARY YEAR OF THE NATIONAL HUNT COMMITTEE WHICH WHEN INAUGURATED IN 1866 WAS KNOWN AS THE

GRAND NATIONAL STEEPLECHASE COMMITTEE

TAKING ITS NAME FROM

THE GRAND NATIONAL STEEPLECHASE

THE WORLD FAMOUS RACE WHICH ALTHOUGH IT HAS MANY IMITATIONS HAS NEVER BEEN EQUALLED AND STILL REMAINS THE SUPREME TEST FOR HORSE AND RIDER — ONCE AGAIN IT CAN BE SEEN IN THE SPRING OF

1967

APRIL 6th THURSDAY: THE TOPHAM TROPHY STEEPLECHASE
APRIL 7th FRIDAY: THE LIVERPOOL SPRING CUP
THE MILDMAY STEEPLECHASE

APRIL 8th SATURDAY

THE GRAND NATIONAL STEEPLECHASE

A typical Topham Christmas Card from the 1960s. The 1966 race was won by Anglo and the 1967 race by the 100/1 outsider Foinavon. Incidentally, these Christmas Cards were like normal postcards and Mrs Topham sent them out without putting them in envelopes.

The
World Famous Figure
sending the
Annual Ancient Wish
to All from
The Ancient Chair
on the
World Famous
Steeplechase Course
at
Aintree

THE CHAIR A RELIC OF BYGONE DAYS Occupied by the Distance Judge who 'retired' horses failing on a time limit or were out-distanced when the Winner had passed the WInning Post. Believed to be the only one extant and now remembered only by the Judqe's decision, 'Won by a distance'

A Merry Christmas and All Good Going in 1968

The inscription in green under the picture which is very hard to read is:- "THE CHAIR - A RELIC OF BYGONE DAYS - Occupied by the distance Judge who 'retired' horses failing on a time limit or were out-distanced when the Winner had passed the Winning Post. Believed to be the only one extant and now remembered only by the Judge's decision, 'Won by a distance'."

Grand National Day 1961, my son Geoffrey with Russian jockeys B Ponomarenko and V Prakhov who rode Reljef and Grifel respectively. Both horses were trained by Boris Alexiev who I met again at the Pardubice in Czechoslovakia in 1991.

The Chair in 1961. The grey is the winner, Nicolaus Silver, ridden by Bobby Beasley. Nicolaus Silver was trained by Fred Rimell at Kinnersley in Worcestershire. Just behind the winner is Fred Winter with hooped sleeves and a diamond on Kilmore. They were to win the next year.

betting lists, being ousted from favouritism shortly before the 'Off' by Leopardstown Chase winner, and the mount of Pat Taaffe, Jonjo. In the fast run race, Liverpool owned Fresh Winds blazed a front-running trail for the whole of the first circuit, during which both the Russian horses came to grief. Grifel was remounted after his tumble at Bechers, only to be pulled up after the water jump when a long way behind the main bunch of survivors. At Bechers second time round, Merryman II, this year partnered by Derek Ancil, was showing every likelihood of bringing off a double not achieved in the National since 1936. But always in close attendance was the attractive grey Nicolaus Silver and, taking the lead at the penultimate fence, he was ridden out for a decisive five length victory by jockey Bobby Beasley, to become the first grey to win the race for ninety years. With Merryman II the runner-up and O'Malley Point and Scottish Flight II filling the minor places of the fourteen finishers, there was overwhelming agreement that the modification of the fences had made the event much fairer. Kinnersley trainer Fred Rimell celebrated his second National win far more conclusively than his first with E.S.B., and as with that horse, my own small domain of Paddock Yard played a small part in the success. At morning gallops it had been discovered that Rimell's team had mislaid the hoof oil needed for Nicolaus Silver's feet. The best I could offer Fred's travelling head lad Jack Kidd as a substitute was a can of Castrol engine oil left over from the last motor racing fixture, yet it proved as effective with the horse as for its true purpose.

Security at Aintree had always been most stringent during big race week but in 1962, after death threats to jockey Bobby Beasley, the activity of the police and private agents was extremely noticeable. The jockey's mount, Nicolaus Silver, had progressed in great heart since last year, with victories in Liverpool's Grand Sefton and a scintillating performance in Doncaster's Great Yorkshire Chase; although only joint third favourite on the day, too much money for some people's comfort had been laid for a repeat performance. Top spot in the betting, at 7/1, rested with the brilliant seven year old, Frenchman's Cove, a son of the 1946 Derby winner Airborne.

Despite the very soft going and atrocious weather conditions, the first half of the race was surprisingly trouble-free, with only three missing from the field as they went back into the country for the final time. From here on though, it became a test of stamina, and at the post it was Fred Winter on Kilmore who secured the prize by ten lengths from the other two twelve year olds. Previous winners Nicolaus Silver and Merryman II were among the seventeen who completed the course, an amount like last year which endorsed the wisdom of modifying the fences.

If Aintree's most famous event appeared to at last have met with general approval, it was becoming obvious that, apart from the Autumn Grand Sefton meeting, the other fixtures at Liverpool were growing less popular. A distinct shortage of runners at these was giving much cause for concern.

In 1963, forty-seven runners, the largest number for eleven years, went to the post, with Frenchman's Cove heading the handicap with twelve stone and Kilmore, Nicolaus Silver and Mr. What each returning to the scene of their greatest glory. Neville Crump's only representative, Springbok, was the 10/1 favourite, while many housewives looked no further

Recently my daughter Barbara and my grandson Jimmy pose outside Team Spirit's stable. Jimmy was born during Team Spirit's winning round - March 21st 1964.

Above: Lord Oaksey, then The Hon. John Lawrence, lands in fine style amongst fallers after The Chair in the 1964 race won by Team Spirit.
The previous year John had been beaten 3/4 of a length when riding Carrickbeg, by the Keith Piggott trained Ayala.Lord Oaksey and Dick Francis, who was also second as a rider on Roimond in 1949, were wonderful with their pens in helping to save our great Liverpool race.

Left: Major Headley-Dent, Inspector of Courses, measures The Chair before the 1985 race, I am in the ditch with Hugo Bevan. I am very fond of Hugo and was sad when he left Aintree. Lord Oaksey, when he was riding, on one occasion accused me of building the fences too high but as you can see they are very carefully measured!

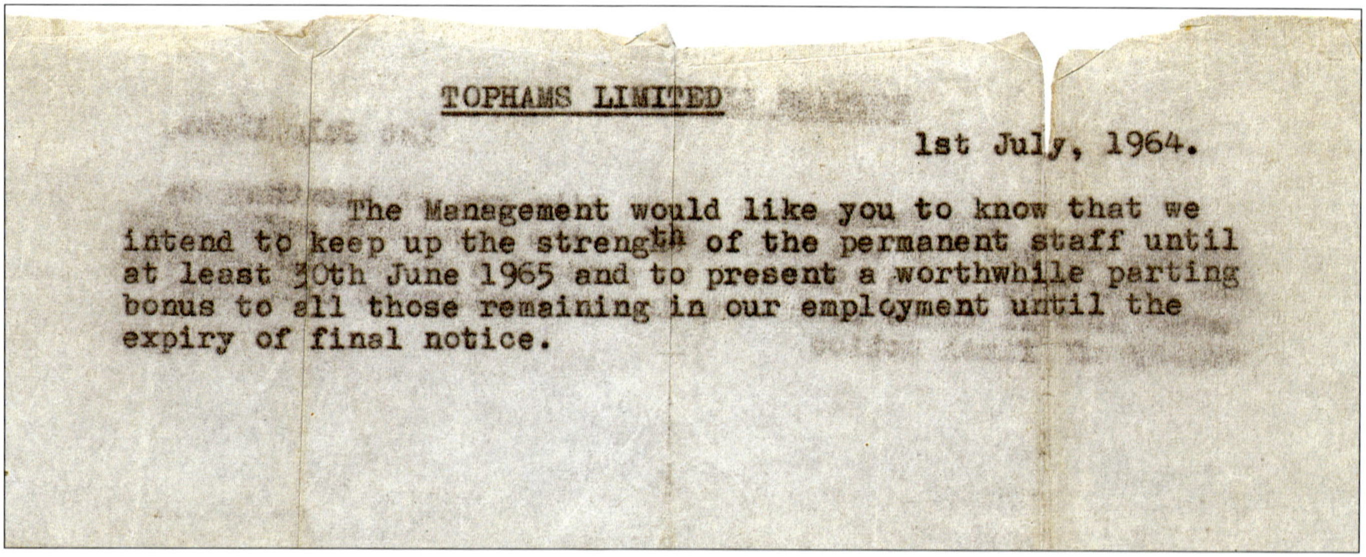

TOPHAMS LIMITED

1st July, 1964.

The Management would like you to know that we intend to keep up the strength of the permanent staff until at least 30th June 1965 and to present a worthwhile parting bonus to all those remaining in our employment until the expiry of final notice.

Above: My first redundancy notice back in 1964 from the Tophams. The bonus mentioned in this note got paid in 1974! I had expected between £50 and £100 and when I opened the letter enclosing the cheque I thought that it was for £100 which would have been very acceptable. I left it out for my wife to pay into the bank and she rang me saying that it was for £1,000, certainly Mrs. Topham "looked after her own".

Right: I think my last redundancy notice but we were saved by the Jockey Club.

AINTREE RACECOURSE

Famous for the Grand National

AINTREE RACECOURSE CO. LTD.

AINTREE, LIVERPOOL 9 5A5 TELEPHONE 051-523 2600

RNF/ES

22nd October 1982

Mr. H. O. Dale,
22 Oakhill Drive,
Lydiate,
Liverpool L31 2LF

Dear Mr. Dale,

I am writing to you on the subject of your employment by Aintree Racecourse Company Limited following the staff meeting which was held at the Racecourse on Tuesday, 12th October 1982.

I very much regret to have to advise you that your employment by this Company cannot continue after 31st October 1982, the date stipulated in our letter of 12th May 1982 but, if circumstances change in time, we would hope to be able to review this position.

for a flutter than to Hollywood actor Gregory Peck's Irish trained grey, Owen's Sedge.

The contest proved to be one of the most exciting seen for many years, with the highly talented Josh Gifford on the free-running Out and About cutting out all the running in very flamboyant fashion. It was only after he fell four out that the race appeared wide open, with Hawa's Song, Springbok, Kilmore, Ayala, Owen's Sedge and the seven year old Carrickbeg all with a winning chance. Coming into the last fence, amateur The Hon. John Lawrence took Carrickbeg to the front, a position they held till well past the elbow. Only in the dying strides of the race did the result appear in question, when, from seemingly nowhere the 66/1 outsider Ayala came with one final flourish to snatch victory by three-quarters of a length. Five lengths further back came Hawa's Song in third place, just ahead of the fast finishing Team Spirit.

For John Lawrence there was only the heartbreak experienced by so many other gallant riders through the years in the quest for National glory. Ayala's jockey, Pat Buckley, on the other hand, wore the victor's mantle well remembering no doubt his premature exit from last year's race when falling with Springbok at the very first fence. It was also a moment to savour for winning trainer Keith Piggott, whose son Lester had brought new meaning to flat-race record breaking. Keith's father was the great Aintree jockey Ernie.

It was at the Yuletide meeting in December 1963 when the clouds of tragedy once more cast their shadow across the Liverpool racecourse, and indeed the whole world of National Hunt racing. That magnificent horseman and absolute credit to his profession, Tim Brookshaw, crashed through the wing of the fifth flight in the Holly Handicap Hurdle when his mount Lucky Dora swerved when leading. The accident occurred far away from the treacherous ditches and brooks the brave and always genial Brookshaw had so many times mastered; yet racing lost one of its most worthy ambassadors when it was discovered that the thirty-four year old jockey had broken his back. Equally popular among his weighing room colleagues and racegoers everywhere, Tim's epic stirrup-less ride aboard Wyndburgh four years before would forever remain a tribute to his spirit of determination and total dedication to the sport.

The big day in 1964 began in the worst possible manner, when a light aircraft crashed near the Canal Turn killing all five occupants, including the television personality and journalist Nancy Spain. Further tragedy came in the race itself, with north country jockey Paddy Farrell receiving a broken back through the fall of his mount Border Flight.

Peacetown and Out and About set a hot pace and were still at the head of affairs over the second Valentines. On the run to the final fence, Purple Silk moved to the front with Peacetown, Eternal, Springbok, Pontin-Go and the diminutive Team Spirit all in a line behind and in hot pursuit. It was only in the last one hundred yards that former flat-race jockey Willie Robinson produced a glory winning effort from Team Spirit to pass the post half a length ahead of Purple Silk, with Peacetown a very game third. Winning trainer Fulke Walwyn became with this victory one of an exclusive band of men to both ride and train the big Aintree winner.

In the weeks which followed there came into being a long overdue fund for riders such as Tim Brookshaw and Paddy Farrell, injured in the pursuit of what must surely be one of the most perilous of professions. Thanks to the concern and efforts of such as Clifford Nicholson and Edward Courage, the foundations of the Injured Jockeys Fund were laid and, with such a wise and energetic trustee as John Lawrence, this organisation has provided to this day needs previously neglected.

Even to what Mrs. Topham always described as her small family of faithful staff, there was not the slightest suggestion or hint that anything was other than normal. Even Mrs. Topham's periodic and much appreciated egg and ham bingo suppers for friends and employees went ahead as planned on 1st July 1964, the only slightly unusual variance on that occasion being that we were inexplicably all given the afternoon off that day. It was of course, as we soon discovered, to enable the television people time to pre-record the shock announcement which was to shake the entire racing world.

Through rising costs and with regard to her increasing age, Mrs.'T' had decided to sell the racecourse and had secured a purchaser in secret negotiations, the property company Capital and Counties Ltd. It was like a bolt from the blue for everyone at Aintree, causing severe concern to us all with the likelihood that we would be joining the ranks of the unemployed in an area already long depressed with the horrors of joblessness.

So began the unthinkable realisation that the 1965 Grand National would be the last to be held at Aintree, and although statements were made assuring all that a similar event would take place at Haydock or Doncaster, we at the racetrack and the press in general knew that any such substitute would be a National in name only. The confusing legal arguments pertaining to Lord Sefton's Contract of Sale were to remain through all the wrangling, no comfort to any of us whose future, like that of The Grand National itself, had come to an end.

If the next National was to be the final one in the long and distinguished history of the world's greatest steeplechase, then all of us were determined that it would go out in a never to be forgotten manner. The course and fences received more care and faithful preparation than ever before, our hard work and diligence contradicting the heaviness of heart we suffered.

From the very day the entries for the race were announced, it was apparent that the forthcoming event would be appropriate to a most memorable if sad racing moment. Her Majesty The Queen Mother attended Aintree to watch her consistently good park chaser The Rip attempt what Devon Loch had so narrowly failed to do. As a spectacle the 1965 Grand National was as exciting and full of drama as any in my time. It developed into a match between the pride of Scotland, Freddie, and the American challenger, Jay Trump, with both their jockeys riding a finish from a long way out. Despite crashing through the final fence, Jay Trump came away from it a length to the good but with Freddie galloping all the way to the line, it was as thrilling a finish as anyone could ever hope to see. At the post Jay Trump prevailed by three-quarters of a length, with Mr. Chris Collins twenty lengths back in third place on his recently purchased Mr. Jones. For victorious

Entries from my stable book showing boxes 1-24/5 in Paddock Yard for the Grand National Meetings of 1965 and 1966. The 1965 race went to the Fred Winter trained Jay Trump who arrived on the Thursday and left on the Sunday and the 1966 race also went to one of Fred's horses Anglo who had the same box and who also arrived on the Thursday and left on the Sunday. Fred's last four rides in the great race were all on Kilmore trained by Ryan Price. In 1961 they were fifth, in 1962 they won, in 1963 they were sixth and in 1964 Kilmore fell.

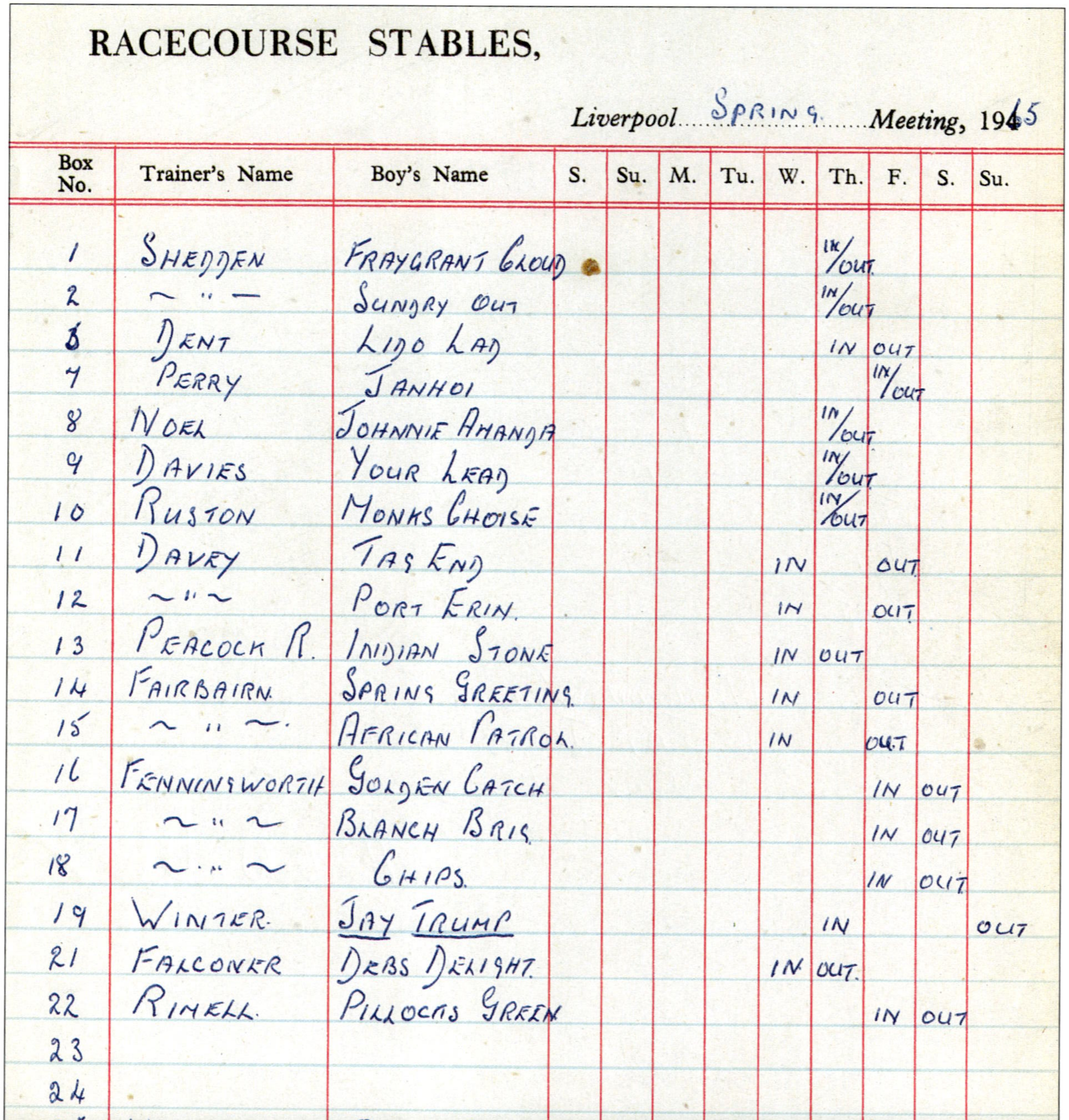

RACECOURSE STABLES,

Liverpool SPRING *Meeting*, 1965

Box No.	Trainer's Name	Boy's Name	S.	Su.	M.	Tu.	W.	Th.	F.	S.	Su.
1	SHEDDEN	FRAYGRANT CLOUD						IN/OUT			
2	~ " —	SUNDRY OUT						IN/OUT			
3	DENT	LIDO LAD						IN	OUT		
4	PERRY	JANHOI							IN/OUT		
8	NOEL	JOHNNIE AMANDA						IN/OUT			
9	DAVIES	YOUR LEAD						IN/OUT			
10	RUSTON	MONKS CHOISE						IN/OUT			
11	DAVEY	TAS END					IN		OUT		
12	~ " ~	PORT ERIN.					IN		OUT		
13	PEACOCK R.	INDIAN STONE					IN	OUT			
14	FAIRBAIRN.	SPRING GREETING.					IN		OUT		
15	~ " ~.	AFRICAN PATROL.					IN		OUT.		
16	FENNINGWORTH	GOLDEN CATCH							IN	OUT	
17	~ " ~	BLANCH BRIG.							IN	OUT	
18	~ " ~	CHIPS.							IN	OUT	
19	WINTER.	JAY TRUMP						IN			OUT
21	FALCONER	DEBS DELIGHT.					IN	OUT.			
22	RIMELL.	PILLOCKS GREEN							IN	OUT	
23											
24											

RACECOURSE STABLES, Paddock Yard

Liverpool March *Meeting*, 1946

Box No.	Trainer's Name	~~Boy's~~ Name	S.	Su.	M.	Tu.	W.	Th.	F.	S.	Su.
1	Murphy	Brown Diamond						IN			OUT
2	Legget	Para Handy							IN/OUT		
6	Hall W	Pin Fast						IN/OUT			
7	"	Chancer						IN/OUT			
8	"	Castle Falls						IN/OUT			
9	Grossman	Rustic Ale						IN/OUT			
10	Moore D L	Flying Wild						IN			OUT
11	"	Gale Force X						IN			OUT
12	"	Glyyn Part						IN			OUT
13	Fairbairn	Perilous Gold						IN	OUT		
14	"	El Geza						IN	OUT		
15	Winter	Irish Rebel					IN	OUT			
16	Fairbairn	Ivernaid					IN		OUT		
17	"	Roe Gemmel					IN			OUT	
18	"	Golden Metal					IN			OUT	
19	Winter	Anglo						IN			OUT
20	"	Lifeboat					IN	OUT			
21	McCartan	Dry Don					IN	OUT			
22	Rimell	Dicey						IN/OUT			
23	"	Game Keeper						IN/OUT			
24	"	Fulmanate						IN/OUT			

rider Tommy Crompton Smith it was a moment to treasure, as the first amateur to succeed in the race since Bobby Petre in 1946; for Fred Winter an exceptional beginning to his new career as a trainer; and for the racing public the faint hope that such a valuable piece of our sporting heritage would somehow be saved.

Although our boss was emphatic that the racecourse must be sold, we were allowed to prepare for another season's activities and, even allowing for the uncertainty surrounding the venue, there was no shortage of runners for the autumn meeting which for the first time was only a two day affair. It was Freddie again though, when March came round, who was all the rage with punters, being backed down to a ridiculous 11/4 first choice of forty-seven runners. Unbeaten in his last five outings, What A Myth also came in for heavy support. Almost totally overlooked among the outsiders was Fred Winter's representative Anglo, whose jockey Tim Norman was involved in a car crash near the racecourse the evening before the race.

A treat for many of the large crowd on National day was the appearance among them of the Beatles, the Liverpool pop-group who were taking time off from their globe-trotting to watch Paul McCartney's father's horse Drakes Drum contest the six furlong Hylton Handicap, the race before the main feature. In a blanket finish, the Cheshire trained five year old got up in the final strides for a shock victory which must have made the 'Fab Four' want to break into song. It could well have been an indication of the further surprise which followed barely an hour later. The favourite, Freddie, was always well in touch, Pat McCarron holding him up for a late challenge. But Anglo had been making steady progress from the nineteenth and coming back onto the racecourse Tim Norman sent the eight year old to the front. Drawing away up the straight, Anglo ran out an easy twenty length winner from Freddie. Justifiably Fred Winter received much praise for turning out two National winners in his first two years as a trainer and, to further endorse his skill, he finished the season third in the winning trainers' list behind Ryan Price and Tom Dreaper.

For the first time in the long history of Aintree, racing at the course was confined to just one meeting in 1967, a fact which to all of us employed there indicated that the time had surely come to seek a more secure future elsewhere. Having lost the last autumn meeting also meant of course that there was little Liverpool form by which to gauge likely prospects for what again was being dubbed the last Grand National of all. Honey End, from the powerful Ryan Price stable, was a worthy 15/2 favourite, having won six times that term. Others who caught the eye were Gregory Peck's Different Class, Bassnet and Kilburn. Trying to repeat last year's success was Anglo, this time partnered by Bobby Beasley, and Freddie was once more in the line-up, but with torrential rain making things difficult for all concerned, it was to prove a day when reputations, past form and quality counted for little.

How the unconsidered Foinavon became the fourth 100/1 shot to achieve National recognition has been shown many times on television re-runs, that dreadful pile-up at the twenty third fence always highlighting the menace of loose horses in any race. Still it must be said that jockey John Buckingham kept a cool head when finding himself suddenly and incredibly left in the lead so far from home. Although

John Buckingham jumps the last on the 100/1 outsider Foinavon in 1967 to victory.

confirming the unpredictability of Liverpool's famous event, it was the worst possible incident which could have happened at a time when such dreadful uncertainty hung over the National.

Thankfully there was no such adverse criticism attached to the race twelve months later, when on a perfect spring afternoon forty-five runners provided a classic spectacle of steeplechasing excitement. That the first four home were all popular fancies satisfied everyone that the Grand National had been won on merit, with last year's unlucky third placed Red Alligator performing brilliantly under Brian Fletcher. The twenty length winning margin Red Alligator held over Moidore's Token, Different Class and Rutherfords suggested that jockey Fletcher could well be right in his belief that, but for the pile-up last year, they would have beaten Foinavon easily.

Although Mrs. Topham's original intended purchaser had apparently lost interest in acquiring the racecourse for development, there were a number of other would-be buyers, all with their intentions clearly set on extensive building at Aintree. The question of planning permission being granted was of course questionable, yet as we prepared in early 1969 for yet another 'final' Grand National, there came an unexpected glimmer of hope. Liverpool Corporation made known its wish to purchase the course for a figure said to be in the region of £1 million, together with the encouraging pledge that if successful they would allow racing to take place at the site. Sadly, by now the public in general were becoming increasingly bored with the whole affair and, even more ominously, within racing a number of racecourses had already drawn up plans to accommodate a substitute National within their fixture list. With just one meeting a year now, it was obvious to us all that the situation was very serious.

For Toby Balding's charge Highland Wedding, the 1969 race was to be a third and final attempt but at now twelve years old many observers considered his best days behind him. There could be no denying though, that the Ayrshire bred gelding was enjoying a new lease of life, with three wins from his last three outings and, when substitute jockey Eddie Harty carried off the Topham Trophy Chase with the Balding trained Dozo just two days before the National, a Liverpool double appeared possible. The B.B.C. improved on their already excellent television coverage of the event by this year for the first time transmitting the proceedings in colour, a most welcome innovation for stay at home viewers. Always well up with the pace, Highland Wedding jumped well throughout, took up the running from the Richard Pitman ridden long time leader Steel Bridge at the second Canal Turn to win convincingly by twelve lengths. Steel Bridge was second, in front of Rondetto, The Beeches and Josh Gifford on Bassnet, with nine others managing to complete the course. The winner's reward was a well earned retirement to his owner's home in Canada, while Eddie Harty could proudly reflect that he had become the only man to represent his country, Eire, in an Olympic three day event and then ride the winner of the Grand National.

Valentines 1969, the winner Highland Wedding ridden by yet another great Irish jockey E.P. Harty, just leads Richard Pitman, who gave me this signed photograph, on the second Steel Bridge. Richard was a top class jockey around Aintree and was also second on Crisp in 1973. His son Mark was second in the 1991 race on Garrison Savannah having won the Gold Cup two or three weeks earlier.

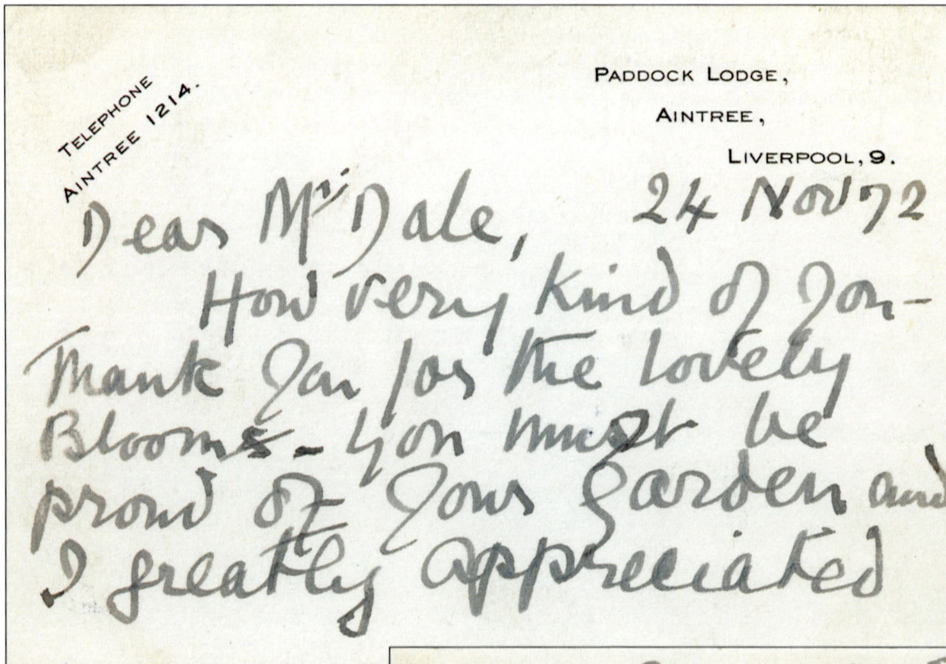

TELEPHONE
AINTREE 1214.

PADDOCK LODGE,
AINTREE,
LIVERPOOL, 9.

24 Nov 72

Dear Mr Dale,
How very kind of you -
Thank you for the lovely
Blooms - You must be
proud of your garden and
I greatly appreciated

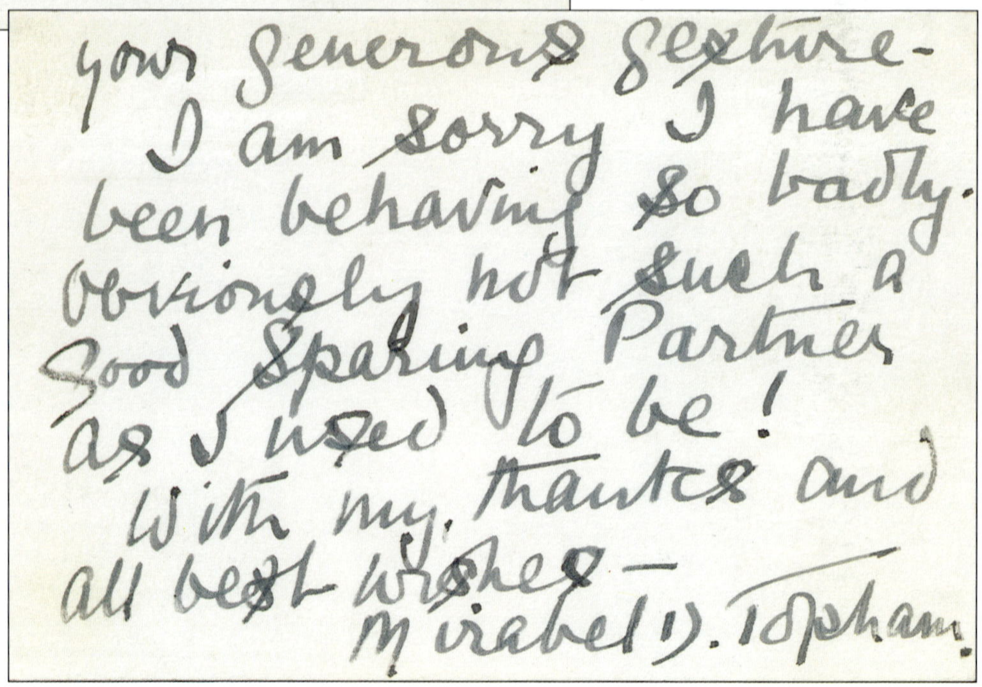

your generous gesture -
I am sorry I have
been behaving so badly.
Obviously not such a
good Sparring Partner
as I used to be!
With my thanks and
all best wishes -
Mirabel D. Topham.

A nice handwritten card from 'Mrs. T' thanking me for a bunch of flowers which I had given her.

The 1970's

It was with sadness that we awaited the seasonal course inspection in 1970, for Major Gilbert Cotton was retiring immediately after performing the task he had so cheerfully and efficiently carried out for the last half century. He had always been a most popular man with everybody, full of good humour and a knowledge of the jumping game which he had served so excellently since riding The Rejected IV in the 1913 Grand National. It was a typically kind gesture when Mrs. Topham presented him with a silver cigarette box upon completion of his final examination of the course.

Of the twenty-eight runners for this year's big race, local trainer George Owen supplied the favourite in the form of the 13/2 shot Two Springs. Red Alligator was back again, along with Rondetto and The Beeches but Dozo and Fred Rimell's Welsh National winner French Excuse were the most heavily backed after the favourite. As usual Mr. Rimell selected my domain Paddock Yard for his runners and on this occasion it was interesting to note the Kinnersley maestro had a very useful looking second string for the National. Gay Trip had begun the season in blistering fashion with a win first time out in Cheltenham's Mackeson Gold Cup and his rider Terry Biddlecombe had always expressed the view that the son of Vulgan would make a perfect Aintree type. Unable to take the ride at Liverpool because of injury, Terry suggested to his guvnor that the renowned horseman Pat Taaffe would make the ideal substitute. And so it was, that the forty year old Irishman went out for one last tilt at the big fences, in what he had previously announced was to be his final season in the saddle. Another who had decided to hang up his boots after this race was the four times champion jockey Josh Gifford, whose mount Assad was saddled by a man now better known for flat racing success, Guy Harwood.

After Bechers second time there was only a handful left standing and it was from this point that we were treated to a masterful example of supreme jockeyship. Pat Taaffe was at his most brilliant best, restraining Gay Trip in fourth or fifth place, picking exactly the best place to jump and at the second last, moving smoothly into the lead. No more fitting conclusion to any jockey's career could have been seen anywhere than on that Aintree afternoon, when Pat Taaffe brought Gay Trip majestically over the final fence and, with those perfect hands and heels, raced clear for a very decisive twenty length victory. The second horse Vulture was trained by Taaffe's usual boss Tom Dreaper, with another Irish challenger, Miss Hunter, in third place just ahead of Dozo. The first five jockeys were all Irishmen.

With still no buyer for the racecourse in sight and Liverpool Council dragging their heels while yet declaring an interest, we slogged on with our day to day chores, hoping against hope that some miracle would remove that terrible question mark which had hung over us all for too long. The only encouragement forthcoming from the Jockey Club was the granting of Aintree's solitary fixture per season.

Gay Trip paid a harsh penalty for his convincing National win, the handicapper placing him at the head of the weights with 12 stone, but still only nine years of age and re-united with the charismatic Terry Biddlecombe, wound up 8/1 favourite for a repeat success in 1971. That popular owner Mr. Jim Joel had been trying for many years to capture the Aintree prize and, represented this time by his classy park chaser The Laird, beaten only a neck three years before in the Cheltenham Gold Cup, it looked likely that this could well be his year. Others among the thirty-eight runners who caught the public's attention were Tom Dreaper's exciting duo Vulture and Black Secret. The latter, winner of six of his eight starts this term, was the mount of the trainer's amateur son Jim Dreaper, a most accomplished horseman and worthy assistant to his father. Right from the start the shocks and spills came fast and furiously, with Gay Trip blundering his way out at the very first fence and The Laird exiting two jumps later. The ever popular Ron Barry led over the final fence with Sandy Sprite; there was every possibility that she would become the first of her sex to succeed for twenty years. Still in front at the elbow, she battled on gamely as Black Secret passed her. Squeezing through on the rails with barely two hundred yards to go, John Cook produced his mount Specify with a devastating run to snatch the result almost on the line by a neck from Black Secret, with Astbury and Bowgeeno following. The lightly raced Epsom trained winner was led-in by his ecstatic owner, holiday camp king Fred Pontin, who declined to confirm if it was his money which had brought Specify's price down five points to 28/1 shortly before the start.

There was a highly promising and most unexpected development in the tedious on-off saga of Liverpool racecourse in 1972, with the news that, thanks to generous sponsorship from Messrs. B.P., the latest National would be the most valuable ever. A first prize of £25,765 attracted a field of forty-two, but more importantly an outstanding Irish gelding, who though but still a nine year old, was already the winner of two Cheltenham Gold Cups. Owned by wealthy American Raymond Guest, L'Escargot was handled by Dan Moore, who as a jockey in 1938 had experienced the heartbreak of Aintree defeat when going under by a mere head on Royal Danieli. Not even L'Escargot's top weight of 12 stone could deter the public from supporting him to 17/2 favouritism, ahead of Gay Trip, Cardinal Error, Black Secret and Fair Vulgan. For the current champion jockey Graham Thorner, there was something of a melancholy purpose attached to his partner in the race, Well To Do. Upon the tragic death of Well To Do's owner, Mrs. Heather Sumner, the previous summer the horse had been left in that lady's will to the man who had cared for the animal since its early years, Captain Tim Forster. Only a last minute decision had persuaded the Letcombe Basset trainer to submit his inheritance to the rigours of Liverpool's big chase.

Jim Dreaper, now in command at Kilsallaghan through the retirement of his legendary father, watched from the trainers' stand as his Black Secret, in the capable hands of Sean Barker, gave a faultless display of jumping among the leaders from the 'Off'. L'Escargot was baulked and knocked over at the first ditch.

Black Secret, Gay Trip, the outsider General Symons and Well To Do jumped the last in line abreast, but in driving rain Well To Do stayed on the stronger,

At Wem in Shropshire,
my wife Joan flanked by Ted Mathews
and his wife Minnie;
he was Mrs. Topham's Dairyman
for many years.

1972, discussing security with Jimmy Scott, an excellent friendship still exists, just one of the many friends I made at Aintree.

taking full advantage of his twenty-two pounds from Gay Trip to win by two lengths. Black Secret and General Symons were declared to have dead-heated for third place.

If the sponsorship of the most recent Grand National had infused our flagging spirits with just a modicum of hope, the terrific news we received just three months later lifted us as high as the Liver Birds. Somehow we had been granted an autumn fixture. Held on the last Saturday in October 1972, it was just a one day affair but everyone felt it was a much needed step in the right direction and I personally felt a deep debt of gratitude to the companies who had so magnificently come to our aid when too many people considered Liverpool races a poor joke. The B.P. Steeplechase over the Mildmay course was most fittingly won by Her Majesty The Queen Mother's Inch Arran. Of the three flat races, The Burton Mile was the feature event with prize money donated by the Burton Tailoring Group, but the reason the television cameras were present was the resumption of what we had so missed preparing for the Grand Sefton Chase. Although the name had been changed to the William Hill Grand National Trial, we still thought of it as the 'Sefton', proudly building the big fences in the time honoured fashion. Even the quality of the competitors made the occasion special, with L'Escargot topping the betting from Black Secret, Sunny Lad and Specify. If it was to be the beginning of a fresh period of hope for all associated with the racecourse, then the result could certainly be said to have indicated that; the outsider Glenkiln making all the running to beat L'Escargot easily for the then little known local trainer Donald McCain from nearby Southport.

If few people had heard of 'Ginger' before that crisp autumn day, the whole sporting world knew of him just five months later. The one time taxi driver cum car salesman had fame thrust upon him through his spectacular restoration to fitness of Red Rum. A patient, trusting owner, Mr. Noel le Mare, the unconventional training gallops of Southport's beaches and perhaps the invigorating breezy air from the Irish Sea, all played some part in the racing fairytale which was about to unfold in the toughest sporting arena in the world.

Once more benefiting from B.P.'s sponsorship, the 1973 Grand National was run on the last day of March, and attracted thirty-eight runners together with a huge crowd of spectators intent on seeing some of the brightest stars of the jumping game. Sharing top weight of twelve stone with the Irish ace L'Escargot was Sir Chester Manifold's Australian champion Crisp, prepared for competition in this country by the leading trainer for the last two seasons, Fred Winter. Also with his fair share of weight was Mr. Edward Courage's Spanish Steps with eleven stone thirteen pounds, though as many observed, if ever a horse was bred for the National it must be this, the son of that great mare of the fifties Tiberetta. Ashville, Princess Camilla, Canharis and Black Secret were also in heavy demand in a lively betting market, as was Proud Tarquin, the mount of Lord Oaksey (The Hon. John Lawrence) who two days before had won the Liverpool Foxhunters' Chase with a spirited finish aboard Bullock's Horn. More familiarly known as Mr. John Lawrence, he had of course come so close to National victory ten years before on Carrickbeg.

Surviving a blunder at the first, Crisp quickly opened up a big lead and proceeded to give a superlative exhibition of jumping those notorious fences. At the Chair he was fifteen lengths clear of his nearest rival Endless Folly, with Red Rum tucked in among a cluster of horses lying fifth. Going back to Bechers Crisp's speed and effortless jumping never slackened for an instant and for the first time now, those watching began to realise that this could well be a front-running Aintree performance that would succeed. Fully thirty lengths behind over Bechers, Brian Fletcher also saw the danger that this was one leader who might not come back to them and, setting Red Rum in pursuit, began the seemingly impossible task of catching the runway Crisp. It was only after the last fence, still with a fifteen length advantage, that Richard Pitman detected the first warning signs of distress from his courageous mount, as Crisp veered from his line of progress towards the elbow. With each punishing stride up that never ending run-in Crisp bravely battled on and it was only in the final twenty-five yards that Red Rum caught and passed him for a three-quarter length victory. L'Escargot was a long way back in third place. Lord Oaksey with Proud Tarquin was seventh of the seventeen to finish.

With the disappointing news that there was to be no autumn meeting for us to prepare for, we carried on somewhat dejectedly, dismayed that the latest epic tussle at Aintree had failed to stir the Lords of the Jockey Club or any would-be purchasers of the racecourse. It was perhaps both ironic and at the same time appropriate that it was a Liverpool man, born barely a mile from the course, who hit the headlines in November, 1973 by lashing out a cool £3 million for Aintree and its famous race. Bill Davies had come up the hard way from the back streets of Liverpool, progressing from a joiner and plasterer through the difficult post-war years to become head of his Walton Construction Company in 1960. A big, flamboyant, bearded man, he was intensely proud of his local background and having extended his business interests to property development, undoubtedly considered his acquisition of a major racecourse a most viable enterprise. He was, however, always in his dealings with the racecourse staff most emphatic that the Grand National would forever be run at Aintree and shared our desire to see many more fixtures held at the track. Fully admitting that he had a lot to learn about supervising the successful operation of a racecourse, Mr. Davies threw himself enthusiastically into organising the next National. An executive of his Walton Group, Peter McCardle, became the new Racecourse Manager, Jim Cunningham the foreman and Stevie Westhead remained senior fence builder; and after an absence of seventeen years Major Beckwith-Smith returned as Clerk of the Course.

With no Crisp in the race this time, Red Rum topped the weights with twelve stone, just one pound more than L'Escargot. The former champion amateur Chris Collins was attempting a unique double with his Arthur Stephenson trained Stephen's Society, the pair having five months earlier scored a resounding success in Czechoslovakia's Grand Pardubice Steeplechase. Our new boss, Bill Davies, was even making an effort to win his own prize money with a chestnut named Wolverhampton and Fred Rimell fielded a strong trio in Rough House, Sunny Lad and Rouge Autumn.

For Brian Fletcher it was an armchair ride on Red Rum, with the local horse always prominent and confidently striking the front at Bechers second time

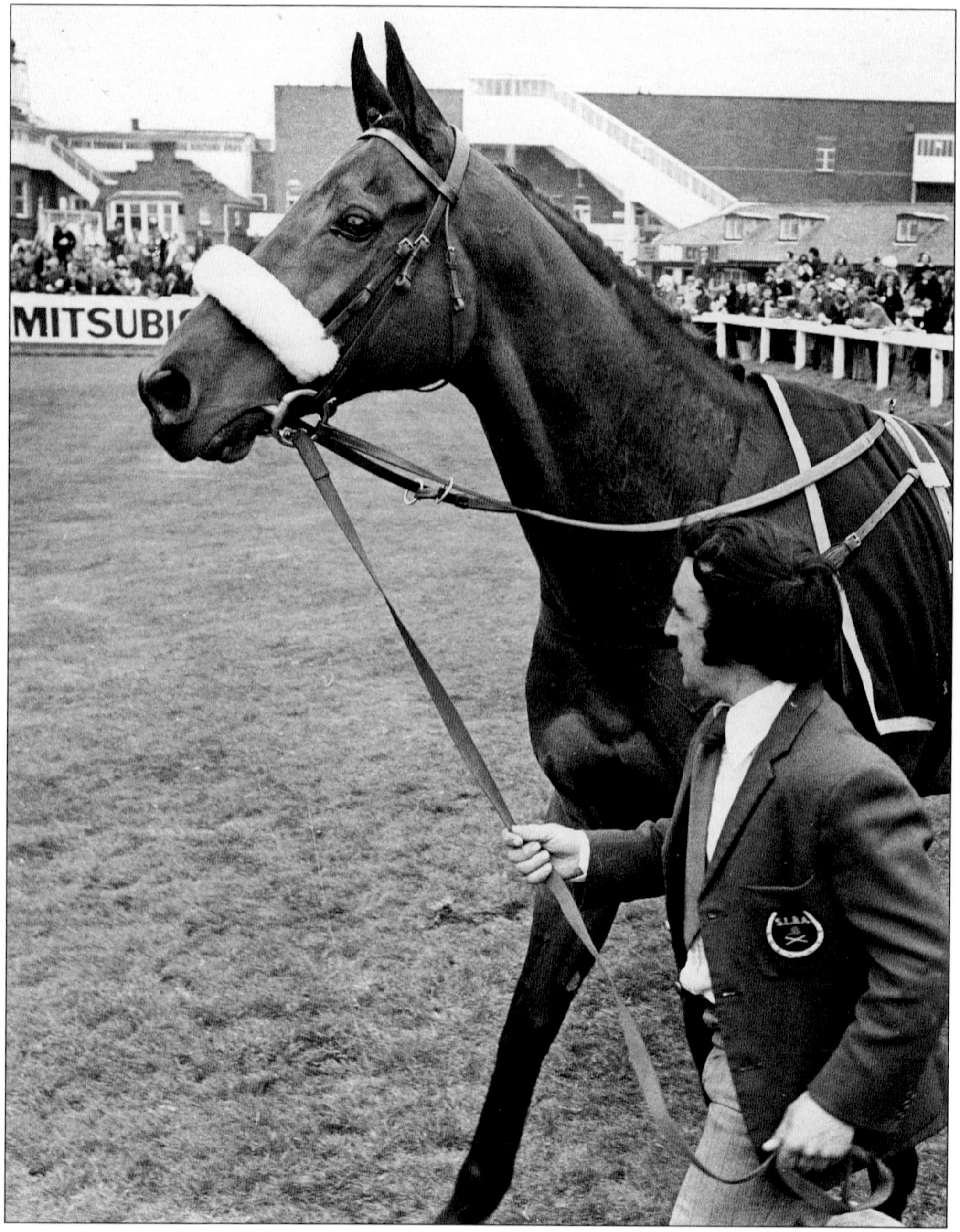

A fine study of Red Rum in the paddock. I have many photographs and pictures of him.

Joan, self and our permanent resident Red Rum in our living room. This lovely painting was presented to me in 1983 at the Holiday Inn.

around. He took the last fence four lengths ahead of L'Escargot; at the post his winning margin had been increased to seven lengths.

Having made last year's critics eat their words, with a clear cut victory which placed him among that elite minority who had succeeded in the world's most demanding race in successive years, Red Rum set the seal on his greatness by turning out a mere three weeks later to win the Scottish Grand National.

Sadly Bill Davies soon lost his image of saviour of Aintree when some hard headed business decisions concerning the National became the subject of fierce criticism from all sections of the media. Even the happy relationship with the B.B.C., nurtured so strenuously by Mirabel Topham, suffered a set-back when certain managerial aids of Mr. Davies suggested that television camera-men should focus more attention on the advertisers' bill-boards situated in great profusion around the course. Worse still came the news that admission charges were to be greatly increased for the 1975 Grand National. It was the last straw for many and not even the prospect of Rummie recording an unbelievable third victory in what, thanks to the involvement of the *News of the World*, would be the richest National ever, could induce the public to succumb to what they considered a dictatorial attitude. In consequence the smallest number of spectators ever turned up at Aintree in the hope of seeing the 7/2 favourite Red Rum create an all time record by beating his thirty rivals.

Receiving a weight advantage of eleven pounds from Red Rum, L'Escargot raced away for a fifteen length victory over the local hero, with Spanish Steps again running on magnificently to finish third in front of Money Market and The Dikler.

Hardly had we had time to tidy up the place than we were hit with yet another bombshell. Unable to acquire the planning permission he so desperately needed, and with the property market in a precarious position, Bill Davies announced he was selling the racecourse to another property developer, the Irishman Patrick McCrea. Once more it was a frustratingly worrying time for us all, with our last remaining hopes resting with the Jockey Club or the Levy Board, or some combination of both. In August Mr. McCrea made it known that he was no longer interested in Aintree and shortly afterwards our faith in the Levy Board was shattered when they offered a derisory £400,000 for the racecourse. Bookmakers Ladbrokes' £1.5 million bid was also lamentably short of what Bill Davies required to merely break even, so we approached another winter of abject uncertainty. More bad news came with the Jockey Club's ultimatum to the Walton Group chief, that unless he reached some sort of agreement by the end of December, Liverpool's fixture would be transferred to Doncaster.

If, as the Duke of Wellington claimed, the Battle of Waterloo was a close run thing then the struggle to save the Grand National most assuredly went to the tightest of photo-finishes with the unexpected intervention of Ladbrokes providing the finest Christmas present any of us could have hoped for. A contract signed on 22nd December, 1975 between Bill Davies and Cyril Stein, Chairman of the bookmaking giants, saved the day and with it our hopes for some kind of future. The agreement was for Ladbrokes to manage racing at Aintree until 1978 with an option for a further four years after that date and, although numerous cynics pointed out that it was merely delaying the inevitable, we viewed the latest development as a most welcome life-line.

John Hughes, who was to be the new Clerk of the Course, displayed a friendly confidence and equally importantly an obvious in-depth knowledge of horseracing. Satisfying themselves that we knew our job, they left us to get on with it, while they exhibited a refreshing professional flair on the marketing and publicity side. Racing against time, with just three months before the 1976 National, the new administrators worked furiously yet efficiently and with a determination which we all found inspiring. John Hughes in particular, whose valuable experience at Lingfield, Epsom and Haydock was the ideal grounding for his latest role, toiled ceaselessly to restore our Aintree to its former glory. His enthusiasm for the place was a joy to see, as was his appreciation of the romance and history which was the lifeblood of the Grand National. That the 'new boys' had performed well was witnessed by all on April Fools' Day, 1976 when the re-vamped Liverpool Spring meeting was unveiled to an incredulous public. Through increased sponsorship for the supporting events, both the quantity and quality of competitors improved dramatically and the experiment to reduce the number of flat races to just four for the entire three days was a resounding success. The opening day saw a new milestone in the Aintree story passed when a charming young lady named Charlotte Brew became the first of her sex to ride over the big fences. Finishing fourth on her own Barony Fort in the Greenall Whitley Foxhunters' Chase she set a pattern which was bound to be copied.

A newly instituted hurdle race, The Templegate, was a more than fitting prelude to the Grand National with the dual Champion Hurdle winner Comedy of Errors beating Grand Canyon by a short head to boost Fred Rimell's hopes of again topping the trainers' list. It was most appropriate that it was the National itself which put the leading trainers' title beyond question, with Fred's perfectly turned out Rag Trade withstanding the brave late challenge of Red Rum to provide a second victory in the race for owner, 'Teasy Weazy' Raymond. Yet again Red Rum had given his all, losing nothing in defeat under his new partner Irishman Tommy Stack, with his former jockey Brian Fletcher once more proving his value at Aintree by coming third on the mare Eyecatcher.

If Ladbrokes' initial stint at managing Liverpool races was an overwhelming success, as even the media's harshest critics agreed it was, then what followed can only be described as superlative. A distinct sense of pride in being part of a dedicated team restored our belief that there still remained people in authority who cared about Aintree and its unique steeplechase. The energy and imagination of John Hughes was simply exhilarating and with such as Mike Dillon and Nigel Payne so diligently marketing our product, the racing world eagerly awaited Aintree's next bill of fare. That the wait was well worth while nobody was left in any doubt, with a climax to the principal event not only fitting the wonderful occasion but one that would live forever in the memories of all fortunate enough to witness it.

The entire fixture for 1977 was devoted to jumping, each hurdle race and steeplechase richly endowed with sponsored prize money to such a

L'Escargot is led back after winning the 1975 race. He had already won two Cheltenham Gold Cups and been third in 1973 and second in 1974 in our great race. His owner Raymond Guest sent the yard at least a crate, if not more, of champagne that happy day.

L'Escargot watches as we start the party outside his box. L'Escargot was trained by the lovely Irishman Dan Moore, who had been second as a jockey on Royal Danieli in 1938 when they were beaten a head by the young Bruce Hobbs on Battleship. As I am in this photo I must have got someone to use my camera.

degree that the quality of competition rivalled that at the Cheltenham National Hunt Festival. In fact the two most recent Cheltenham heroes were part of the Liverpool cast. Night Nurse, having just secured his second Champion Hurdle success, provided the most thrilling contest imaginable when dead-heating with the brilliant Irish entire Monksfield in the Templegate Hurdle in the race before the National. Another Irish invader, Mick O'Toole's Gold Cup champion Davy Lad, was considered by many pundits to be absolutely thrown in the big race with only 10 stone 13 pounds. Fred Rimell kept me very busy in Paddock Yard, fielding a team of four with the 15/2 favourite Andy Pandy, Brown Admiral, The Pilgarlic and Royal Thrust, and among the newer generation of trainers Mrs. Jenny Pitman brought a 200/1 outsider, The Songwriter, all the way from Lambourn. Another of the fairer sex putting herself well and truly into the record books was Charlotte Brew, who as the rider of Barony Fort, became the first woman to ride in the race.

For the fifth consecutive year all eyes were on Red Rum as he led the parade of forty-two runners in front of the stands and, although joint second favourite at 9/1, his position in the market was largely through sentiment. On that bright spring day though, which will remain forever indelibly imprinted on my mind, the brave battler from the Southport sands made a sheer mockery of any form book ever compiled. Tucked in by Tommy Stack among the mid-division in the early stages of the race, Rummy as usual jumped beautifully.

Back from Valentines second time, Rummy gave a completely new meaning to the word brilliant, bowling along in front and jumping with a precision and speed that was breathtaking. What a procession he made of the so often heartbreaking run to the post, Red Rum crossing the line an incredible twenty-five lengths ahead of Churchtown Boy, with Eyecatcher running on best of the remainder to secure third place for the second time.

This was Rummy's last race at Aintree. His record of three wins and two seconds in the Grand National is most unlikely to be equalled. It must also be remembered that he carried top weight of 12 stone to victory in 1974 and was second under the same weight in 1975, the performances of a class horse.

Adding to the managerial strength at Aintree, came Mr. Rod Fabricius as Racecourse Manager and assistant to John Hughes, while the appointment of Mrs. Eileen Smith as secretary provided us with a delightful and highly efficient lady who was never too busy to listen to our moans and groans. Recognition for Steve Westhead's devoted service came with his promotion to Racecourse Foreman and for myself an official position as stable manager, which was a great compliment as well as being the job above all others I most treasured. For at no other time of the year was I happier, than when booking in the horses for a race meeting; allocating trainers their boxes and enjoying the friendly banter of stable lads and girls whose love for horses I shared so much. Now able to devote more time to repairing those stables which needed it and to suggesting ways of improving the facilities for both horses and lads, I entered what were truly my halcyon days at the racecourse.

Feet up in my little den during the winter of 1975/76, in my left hand a mounted plate from L'Escargot and in my right hand a dead champagne bottle which Raymond Guest had sent us.

Left: Charlotte Brew with Barony Fort the day before the 1977 National. She was the first girl to ride in the Grand National and I became great friends of her and her Mother. Charlotte spent much time in my den avoiding the media.

Right: The start of the race and another of my snapshots - Charlotte is fourth from the left.

Right: Red Rum is led away from the unsaddling enclosure after his third win in 1977. He had won in 1973 and 1974 and had been second in 1975 and 1976.

Left: Andy Pandy the 15/2 favourite for the race trained by the great Fred Rimell who fell.

A photocall for the ground staff on a cold January day in 1978 with 'The Boss', Stevie Westhead, at the front - I'm fifth from the front.

Spring 1982, three generations on the staff, my grandson Jimmy (junior) and my son-in-law, Jimmy (senior), and myself by The Chair. See page 31 for the story of The Chair.

As had been the case since the sale of the racecourse, I often encountered Mrs. Topham taking a stroll, for she still owned and sometimes lived at Paddock Lodge. Able to speak with her less formally than before, our chats together were always friendly; she invariably had some wise observations to make and never failed to kindly enquire after the welfare of my family.

Although unfit to compete, Red Rum received a rapturous welcome as he led the 1978 parade, the only sad note coming when he was led back to the stables as the others waited to come under orders.

Coolishall appeared the biggest danger as they jumped the last fence right on the heels of Sebastian V but despite hitting the final two fences quite hard, Lucius came with a late run on the flat to win in a thrilling finish by half a length from Sebastian V, with the fast finishing Irish outsider Drumroan a neck back in third place. Coolishall was a close up fourth just ahead of The Pilgarlic. It was a first success in the race for trainer Gordon W. Richards and also for three times champion jockey Bob Davies who took the mount as a late substitute when David Goulding became injured.

It may have been simple imagination, but in the final run-up to the 1979 Grand National, there really did seem to be far more press photographers than usual about the place.

'The field included two Cheltenham Gold Cup winners Alverton and Royal Frolic but by the time the second last was reached John Francome was racing for home on Rough and Tumble, just ahead of Zongalero, Rubstic and The Pilgarlic. As they safely reached the run-in, another close finish seemed a certainty. With Rough and Tumble tiring beyond the elbow, Zongalero swept to the front only to find Rubstic staying on the stronger on his outside and at the post it was Rubstic by a length and a half.

Rubstic became the first Scottish trained horse to enter the Grand National winner's enclosure and after so many near misses by those from north of the border it was a victory for perseverance. Winning owner John Douglas, the one time British Lion rugby international, was full of praise for his trainer John Leadbetter and also jockey Maurice Barnes, who had been at work from a long way out on the horse which carried him to his greatest triumph.

Amongst the runners strongly fancied at 14/1 was the winner of the Maryland Hunt Cup from the USA, Ben Nevis. He was brought down when hunting round at The Chair but was soon to make his mark!.

Right: A good finish in 1978; Lucius wins from Sebastian V and a fast finishing Drumroan.

9

Mrs Topham dies at 88

Mrs. Topham's Christmas card in 1971. She is flanked by her nephew and niece, the latter carried the Jack Russell named Becher.
All of us who had worked for her missed her very much when she died.
Although she was nearly 90 she was very alert and well informed right to the end.

1980 to 1991

Through constant rain in the weeks before the race, the going for the first National of the eighties was the worst for many years, leading to a number of fancied runners being withdrawn. As a result only thirty horses faced the starter, with Rubstic the 8/1 first choice in the betting from Jer, Zongalero and Rough and Tumble. Setting off at a sensible pace did not prevent an early crop of casualties, while at the rear the twice Maryland Hunt Cup winner Ben Nevis, was the last to jump Bechers Brook.

It was the second circuit which really sapped the energy in the glue-like conditions, with seven of those still standing bowing out at the nineteenth and Zongalero becoming so exhausted he refused the next. After Delmoss fell when jumping alongside Ben Nevis at the second Bechers, it became a long and lonely road home for the American hope. John Francome tried desperately to get on terms between the last two fences, bringing Rough and Tumble within half a dozen lengths of Ben Nevis, but it was the latter who stayed on the better to race clear on the flat for a twenty length win. That old dependable, The Pilgarlic, was third with the only other finisher being Stan Mellor's New Zealand bred Royal Stuart. It was a well earned second success in the race for trainer Captain Tim Forster and a memorable triumph for rider Charlie Fenwick, in so many ways. For Ben Nevis was owned by his father-in-law, Mr. Redmond C. Steward and an even longer link with the race he'd set his heart on winning, stretched back fifty-two years. Fenwick's grand-father Mr. Howard Bruce was the owner of that great American jumper Billy Barton who came so close to winning the 1928 National behind Tipperary Tim.

The months immediately following that 1980 Grand National were for me as bleak and sombre as any I had yet known, with the sudden loss of two very dear friends. Steve Westhead, a pure genius when it came to building fences and John Booth, our trusty maintenance foreman, passed away within weeks of each other. All too soon after this numbing sadness came the further blow that that grand old lady, Mirabel Dorothy Topham had died in her sleep at Aintree's Paddock Lodge after a short illness. It really was hard to believe that she would no longer stop for a chat with us on the frequent strolls she took around the course which she had spent the best part of her life serving. Often a hard and sometimes difficult taskmistress, she won the hearts and the respect of all of us through the kindness and sincerity which emerged from even her darkest moods.

The offer made to me by Rod Fabricius, to take over Stevie's job as racecourse foreman, was one I initially declined, for I was myself approaching retirement age and more than happy to see out my time at Aintree in the place which was my second home, the stables. It was the prompting of our assistant Clerk of the Course Hugo Bevan which eventually persuaded me to rethink my decision. Hugo was a wonderful gentleman, devoted to steeplechasing and more of a friend than the boss he of course was. Finally I accepted the promotion on the condition that it was

Jimmy carries spruce out of the forest at Greystoke, near to Gordon Richards' stables, shoulders always ache at the end of the day.

Below: A number of us start to dress a fence.

I point out the finer points of fence building to Jimmy a few days before his first Grand National on the staff in March 1980.

Good news at last - The Jockey Club saves The Greatest Racecourse and so The Greatest Race in the World in 1982.
Right: Three cheers for The Jockey Club. Stan and my grandson Jimmy lift me high.
Behind us is The Chair fence before the spruce is put on.

Making the film, *Champions*, at Aintree. It was well named as it was based on the story of Bob Champion who overcame cancer to ride Aldaniti, who overcame serious leg problems, to win the 1981 race. Aldaniti was trained by Josh Gifford, a brilliant jockey, who was second in 1967 on Honey End to the fluke winner Foinavon.
Left: John Buckingham, Foinavon's jockey (see page 45 for them winning), applies 'sweat', in fact shaving foam, to one of the horses. John still works in racing as a jockey's valet.

Right: Reg Green's daughter Helen poses with the star of the film John Hurt.

Left : The real jockeys, who were employed to ride the horses in all of the fast scenes, relax with a game of football.

Reminders of happy and unhappy occasions.

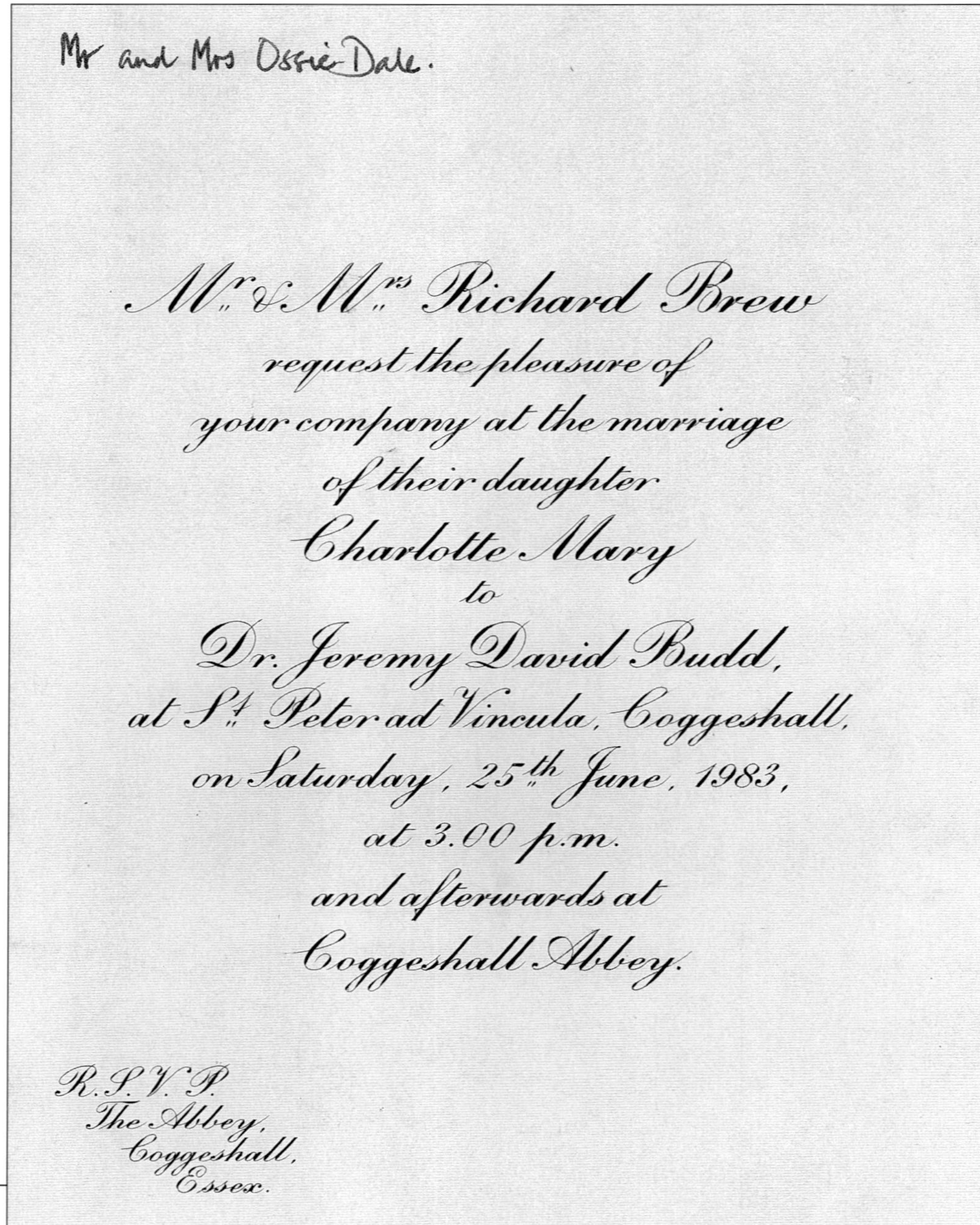

Mr and Mrs Ossie-Dale.

Mr. & Mrs. Richard Brew
request the pleasure of
your company at the marriage
of their daughter
Charlotte Mary
to
Dr. Jeremy David Budd,
at St. Peter ad Vincula, Coggeshall,
on Saturday, 25th June, 1983,
at 3.00 p.m.
and afterwards at
Coggeshall Abbey.

R.S.V.P.
The Abbey,
Coggeshall,
Essex.

ST. DENY'S CHURCH
SEVERN STOKE

†

Thomas Frederick Rimell

JUNE 24th 1913 — JULY 12th 1981

THURSDAY, 16th JULY, 1981

From

F. WALWYN
SAXON HOUSE STABLES

LAMBOURN, BERKS.

Telephone: LAMBOURN 555

To The Stabling Manager,
Racecourse Offices,
Aintree,
Liverpool 9.

22nd March 1984.

Dear Sir,

Please would you reserve six boxes (four straw and two shavings) in the Top Yard as usual. The horses will be arriving in the late afternoon of Wednesday 28th March. Please also reserve accommodation for five lads.

Yours faithfully,

Fulke Walwyn.

One of the nice things about my collection is that I have been able to put various mementoes together. I love the picture of Fulke Walwyn jumping the last to win the 1936 race on Reynoldstown and below a letter from him booking stabling in 1984.

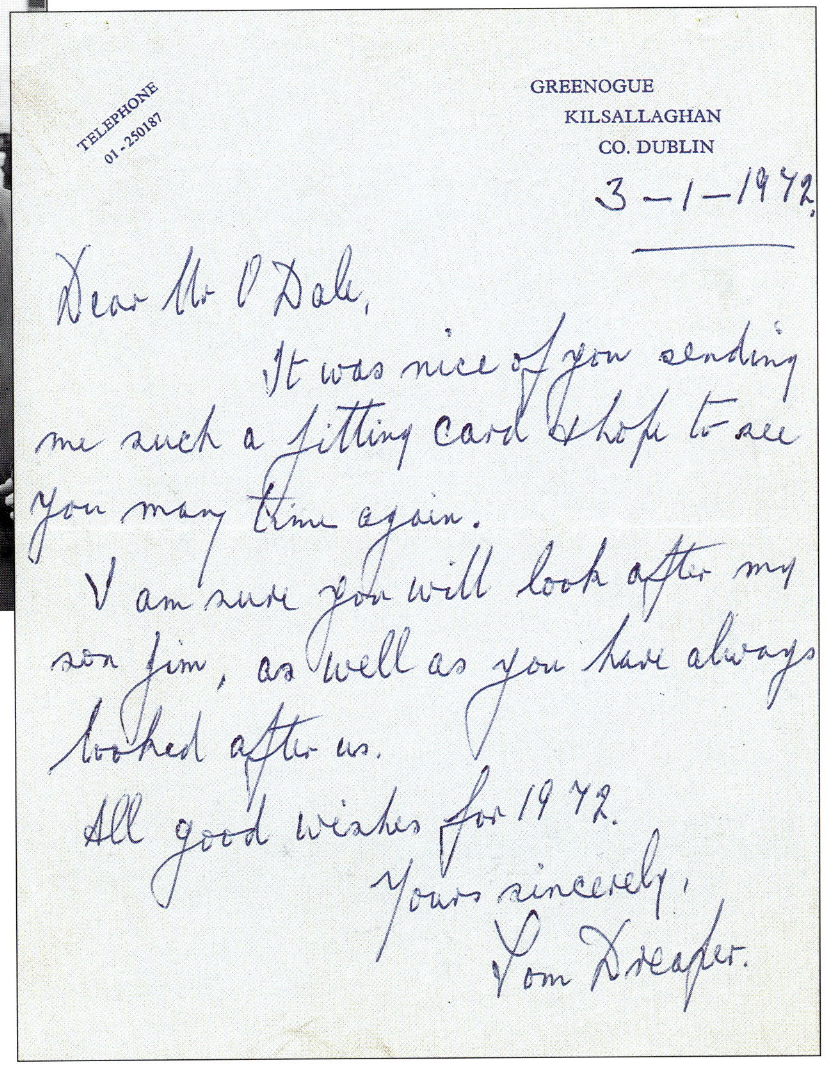

TELEPHONE
01 - 250187

GREENOGUE
KILSALLAGHAN
CO. DUBLIN

3 – 1 – 1972.

Dear Mr O'Dale,

It was nice of you sending me such a fitting card & hope to see you many time again.

I am sure you will look after my son Jim, as well as you have always looked after us.

All good wishes for 1972.

Yours sincerely,

Tom Dreaper.

A letter Tom Dreaper sent me on his retirement in 1972 and a wonderful picture of him and Arkle which one of his lads gave me back in the 1960s. Arkle never ran at Aintree but his owner Anne, Duchess of Westminster is still a regular visitor, and owned Last Suspect, the winner in 1985 (see page 83).

Right: The naming ceremony of the third fence, the first open ditch, in memory of Stevie Westhead in 1982 was performed by Jonjo O'Neill. I wish Stevie was still alive to help with the preparation of this book.

Left: Afterwards Jonjo playing about on the guard rail. Jonjo was a wonderful jockey, although he never won our big race, and has developed into a top trainer of both National Hunt horses and Flat horses.

How not to jump The Chair in 1983; 39 was Canford Ginger and 34 The Vintner.

Jumping Bechers, first time in better style in 1985, the winner was Anne, Duchess of Westminster's Last Suspect, number 11, ridden by H. Davies and trained by Capt. T. Forster.

only until they found someone else and so began my own personal homestretch at Aintree.

It was a truly remarkable time for me and probably the most interesting of all my years at the racecourse. For some strange reason I found that for a couple of weeks each year I was sought out by reporters, radio presenters and even television interviewers. They were all most polite and very eager to discover just what it was about the Grand National that I found so totally absorbing. It is nice to think that maybe a few of them went away with a fuller understanding of what the greatest steeplechase in the world is all about and what it meant for someone like me to be even remotely associated with it.

Meanwhile the job of getting the place ready for another big day went on much as it always has and please God it always shall. A very proud day came for me in August, when my grandson, Jimmy Stevenson, joined the racecourse staff straight from school. Hiding my natural protective instincts, I treated him firmly in those first months, making sure he did more than his share of the mucky unpleasant chores while pointing out the fine traditions we all had to uphold and emphasising that there is never a shortcut to perfection. He, nor anyone else for that matter, could wish for a better introduction to the magic that is the National, than that most emotional of all the 1981 race. Aldaniti and Bob Champion - even the names seem made for each other. A broken down crock of a racehorse and a jockey still fighting bravely to beat cancer. Rising to a challenge as great as the very challenge of life itself and succeeding against the odds in a manner of dignity and inspiration. That simply was the story of the 1981 Grand National, yet like so many others since that far off day when Becher christened the brook, there were others beside the principal players whose loyalty and devotion to a cause made a dream reality. Owner Nick Embiricos, who never for one moment questioned the wisdom of allowing Champion to ride his horse; and that gentlest of all gentlemen, Josh Gifford, a trainer who is a credit to his profession and who in the paddock at Aintree that day, gave the greatest leg-up any jockey ever received. The final word must go to the gallant rider who so nearly shattered the dream, John Thorne, so sporting in defeat on his Spartan Missile and so gracious as the first to shake the hand of the man who beat him.

It was a splendid gesture on the part of Ladbrokes management team when they took the decision to officially recognise the devoted service of my late colleagues Steve Westhead and John Booth, by naming two of the National fences in their honour. That Jonjo O'Neill was chosen to perform the ceremony was most fitting, for he was a man we had all long admired and with whom we had shared many jokes over the years. Steve's favourite obstacle, the third, became the Westhead ditch and the eleventh and twenty-seventh, another open ditch, took the name of John Booth.

A dreadful gap was left in the world of National Hunt Racing when the irreplaceable Fred Rimell died in July 1981, leaving a record of unique service to the sport which would be difficult to equal. On a lighter note, I received a wonderful surprise at the 1982 pre-race press conference, which was yet another display of kind consideration on the part of Aintree's care-taker management team. On behalf of Ladbrokes, Ginger McCain presented me with a silver statuette of a racehorse, a token which takes pride of place in

In the Spring of 1981 I put up Ben Nevis' plaque. Every winner seems to have a glamorous story behind him.

my living room. It was only at this time that the full significance of the forthcoming race really dawned on me, for it was to be the final one under the excellent administration of the Ladbroke organisation. How those seven years had so quickly slipped by.

Painfully once again, the very survival of Aintree became a subject of urgent discussion, but at least this time the Jockey Club became involved in the negotiations. Their plan to purchase the racecourse through the subsidiary Racecourse Holdings Trust, involved a public appeal to raise Bill Davies' asking price of £7 million within seven short months. A daunting task, yet one which appeal chairman, Lord Vestey assured everybody could be achieved through the generosity of the British people. Professional fund-raisers were appointed, Merseyside County Council became involved in a publicity campaign to help and those stalwarts of jump racing, Dick Francis and Lord Oaksey, provided valuable support.

That the 1982 race was to be the richest so far, with the winning owners' reward a tempting £52,507, was surely further evidence that the National was safe. Of the thirty-nine runners it was Frank Gilman's own bred Grittar who started the 7/1 favourite, having run a creditable sixth in the most recent Gold Cup and been a convincing winner of last years Liverpool Foxhunters' Chase. Martinstown and Cheers attracted at least some visual attention due to their very pretty riders Charlotte Brew and Geraldine Rees. Groans of dismay echoed across the course when Aldaniti was seen to be among the ten who departed from the contest at the very first fence and with Bill Smith setting a cracking pace up front on Delmoss, the casualties increased. Taking the shortest way round on Grittar, forty-eight year old amateur Dick Saunders, steered clear of the chaos around him and taking up the running after the second Bechers, ran out a clear fifteen length winner. Hard Outlook was second, the remounted Loving Words a remote third, with long time leader Delmoss fourth and, for the first time ever, a lady rider completed the course. Local lass, Geraldine Rees from nearby Tarleton, slogged on relentlessly to finish last of the eight with Cheers.

The first appeal to save Aintree failed, as we discovered when the November deadline arrived and with Mr. Davies now in dire financial straits, he was left with little choice but to accept a revised offer for his property. Four million pounds was the new target of the latest appeal, but it was an appeal which most certainly did not appeal to the public. A condition of the deal involved the proposed purchaser being allowed to stage the next Grand National, a contingency which thankfully allowed another memorable chapter to be added to the romance filled history of the race. Barely three weeks before the event though, for the only time in my life, I allowed the luxury and foolishness of anger to dictate my actions. Having watched one of our more flamboyant, if eccentric, racing journalists hysterically denounce on television all Liverpudlians as worthless and undeserving of such a great sporting spectacle as the National, I decided to somehow make that 'personality' eat his words. With the aid of many equally irate 'scousers', a sponsored bike-ride was hastily arranged around the racecourse involving myself, as oldest member of Aintree's staff and Jimmy Stevenson as the youngest. Setting ourselves a two hour time limit, the elements frowned on our efforts from the outset, for we rode uncomfortably through a raging blizzard. Housewives, schoolchildren and

The Parade for the 1983 race, led by Grittar ridden by P. Barton. The previous year Grittar had won, when ridden by the Jockey Club member Dick Saunders. Behind Grittar is Mr. Oliver Sherwood on his father's lovely Venture to Cognac who finished eighth and in the green colours is Spartan Missile, ridden by H. Davies. Spartan Missile has been second to Aldaniti in the 1981 race when ridden by his owner/trainer Mr. John Thorne.

many of Liverpool's army of unemployed most generously supported our gesture and the monies raised proudly went off to the appeal headquarters. Typically, although our enterprise was widely publicised in the national press, no retraction was forthcoming from the journalist, who too often refers to the noble creatures which provide him with a lucrative livelihood as 'rags' and 'that thing'.

Having dried out and calmed down, I looked forward to the 1983 race with a new found anticipation, for this one I was determined to see in the flesh. In all my years at Aintree I had only ever watched the race on my portable black and white television from the sanctuary of my Paddock Yard cabin. But this time, I delegated the security of the stables to my grandson Jimmy, with the excuse that the experience of responsibility would do him good. From my position alongside the Chair jump I watched enthralled as Delmoss held his normal position at the head of the field, with Hallo Dandy, Corbiere, Colonel Christy and Grittar in close attendance. The white faced Lambourn trained Corbiere held a two length advantage over the Irish raider Greasepaint over the last, which he quickly increased to twice that distance. Yet in a nail-biting finish, Greasepaint rallied, forcing Ben de Haan to pull out all the stops on Corbiere and hold on for a narrow victory. Another Irish horse, Yer Man, was a poor third, followed home by a tired Hallo Dandy and six others.

If a lady had shared the limelight last year by getting round, a tear stained one stole it in its entirety this time, with Jenny Pitman becoming the first woman ever to train a Grand National winner. And everyone who knows her, agrees whole heartedly that it couldn't have happened to a nicer more genuine person, whose first concern is always the welfare of her horses.

For some six weeks after Corbiere's race the film company Archerwest joined us at the racecourse to make the movie '*Champions*', that incredible story of Aldaniti and his brave jockey.

Terry Biddlecombe was the Technical Adviser and after some initial hair-raising moments, things settled down nicely. The opportunity to renew friendships in a more relaxed atmosphere was greatly welcomed, as was the chance to see such distinguished performers as John Hurt, Edward Woodward, Peter Barkworth and the lovely Jan Francis. Aldaniti was there of course, but by now his poor old legs really had gone and his stand-in for the jumping sequences was Lord Vestey's useful chaser Flitgrove. A heavily made up John Burke doubled for John Hurt in the action shots, with Graham Bradley, Charlie Mann and Chris Pimlott among other jockeys with lesser but equally important roles. Playing himself in the film was the ever amusing John Buckingham, who since his retirement from the saddle had joined his brother Tom as two of the most popular jockeys valets on the circuit.

It was around this time that I was invited to Liverpool's Holiday Inn Hotel one Wednesday afternoon, where hotelier Jack Ferguson, a long time supporter of racing at Aintree, had arranged in conjunction with racing journalist Roy David, a lunch in my honour. Such an exhibition of kind consideration was overwhelming and, together with my wife Joan, daughter Barbara and son Geoffrey, I enjoyed immensely a very proud and moving

1982, Mike Dillon of Ladbrokes (centre) and Donald (Ginger) McCain make my day with a presentation at the pre-race press conference. Mike was smashing to work with and Ginger trained Red Rum.

Right: A spectacular photograph of The Chair in 1983. Jockey P. Double tries to find cover under the fence with Mr. P. O'Connor about to land shoulder first. The leaders by now would have been approaching the water jump.

Far Right: Corbiere, ridden by Ben De Haan and trained by Jenny Pitman, jumps the last in fine style on the way to victory.

Ginger McCain and Geraldine Rees presented me with a framed picture of Corbiere on his way to victory and Merseyside County Council Chairman, James Stuart-Cole with the most wonderful oil painting of Red Rum. Even Mr. Jim Bidwell-Topham attended, along with others of my Aintree friends, including Mrs. Eileen Smith and Frank Dinn.

I shall be eternally grateful to everybody who made that day the marvellous memory it will always be. The only distressing note came later that evening with the news that yet again the attempt to save Aintree had failed. At the eleventh hour the situation was resolved, the Grand National once and for all saved and for the first time in almost twenty years the great race could be enjoyed without the fear that it may be the last. Major Ivan Straker and Seagram stepped forward with sponsorship. Yet to my mind there were two characters just as deserving of plaudits for the priceless contributions they made in bringing to the attention of the world, the unparalleled value of such a race as the National. Through five glorious years Red Rum brought a glowing feeling of well-being to everyone who saw or read of his exploits. In Lord Oaksey, Aintree had a champion whose skill with the written word was akin to that he displayed as a rider and thankfully, when all seemed lost, those words caught the eye of Major Straker. The world of sport owes both a debt of gratitude impossible to repay. Seagram and the newly formed Aintree Racecourse Company did the National proud in 1984, as they have continued to do ever since and although there appeared some new faces to assist the marketing, John Hughes remained as well as many of the old team. Another exciting race, with Penrith trained Hallo Dandy providing a second training success for Gordon Richards, ensured an encouraging introduction for the sponsors, with Greasepaint, Corbiere and Lucky Vane filling the minor places. It was a result popular with the general public especially now that all uncertainty about the race was removed.

Mr. Christopher Collins became a worthy chairman of the company and although it seemed we must soldier on for some time yet with just the one meeting each year, a sense of contentment long missing was welcomed by all. After careful consideration, I decided the time had come for me to call it a day at Aintree, for I was already two years past the official retirement age and realised that younger people deserve the chance to prove themselves. Having made my decision known to the management, I was happy to comply with their suggestion that I stay on in a part-time capacity until a successor could be appointed, and for the next two years my duties involved only two days per week at the course. Except of course for Grand National week, when I slept at the stables for seven nights, a practice I had adopted way back in 1954. My role in the stables for the next two years was purely that of a supervisory one, with my grandson Jimmy running Paddock Yard virtually on his own and I'm pleased to say, in a very able manner.

Last Suspect's late flourish in 1985 won the prize for Anne, Duchess of Westminster, as well as giving Captain Tim Forster a third training success in the race and with Mr. Snugfit second in front of Corbiere and Greasepaint, the outcome was well applauded despite the winner being a 50/1 shot.

My replacement, Bob Dixon, duly arrived and it was with a feeling of pride distinctly tinged with sadness

Richard Dunwoody brings West Tip home by two lengths from Chris Grant on Young Driver in the 1986 race. Twenty lengths behind came Steve Smith Eccles on Classified, followed by P. Tuck on Mr. Snugfit and young Tom Taaffe on Sommelier. Tom's father, Pat, won the race as a jockey in 1955 and 1970 and his grandfather, Tom, trained the winner in 1958.

Left: Enjoying a joke with Geraldine Rees at the launch of the book *Long Live The National* in 1983. Geraldine finished 8th in 1982 on Cheers - still the only woman to have completed the course in the Grand National.

Right: The dustwrapper of my copy of *Long Live The National* in which I have collected many interesting and treasured signatures.

Long Live The
National
John Hughes and Peter Watson
Foreword by H.R.H The Prince of Wales

that I showed him around the place, as I knew that after the next National my employment at the racecourse must end. Bob Dixon settled in well, his earlier role at the now defunct Teeside Park, standing him in good stead for the Liverpool job and when we gave the place a last look round the night before the 1986 Grand National, I admitted to myself with a lump in the throat, that the course had never looked better. Dawn on the big day though, surprised everybody, for during the night a snowfall had left Aintree looking like a scene from a Christmas card. Fortunately the morning sunshine cleared away the snow, but it was still necessary to lay a goodly sprinkling of sand on the landing side of Bechers.

It was the Brook which had brought about the downfall of the well fancied West Tip on the final circuit last year, but this time the nine year old made no mistakes and carrying the jubilant Richard Dunwoody, West Tip beat Scottish trained Young Driver by two lengths. It was as fine a National as anyone could wish to see and for me in particular will always revive memories both marvellous and for obvious reasons, some melancholy. Of the former is the good fortune I had in meeting a gentleman I have grown to admire enormously and also will always be privileged to know as my friend. Vaclav Chaloupka came to Britain in 1986 all the way from his native Czechoslovakia, to partner the horse he trained, Essex, in the National, and although we neither spoke each others language, our shared love of horses somehow overcame all barriers. His small team of assistants became very popular with everyone and despite his exit from the race at the thirteenth due to a broken girth, the promise Vaclav made to one day return was one I just knew he'd keep.

As a final accolade from the racecourse company, the man I had held in such esteem, John Hughes, presented me with one of only three special badges entitling me to lifetime access to all public enclosures at Aintree. My two fellow recipients were David Coleman and Charlie Fenwick and the enamel badge is called the 'Outstanding Services to Aintree Award'.

It was a peculiar feeling for many months afterwards, not having to make that early morning cycle ride to the racecourse, not needing to concern myself with where we could obtain more spruce from and which fences needed to be completely rebuilt this time. Yet the extra time I found myself with allowed me to extend and improve my tiny museum of Aintree history in the spare bedroom. And from January on, each year, I follow avidly the build-up to a new Grand National, with a part of me still longing to be part of the magical scenario.

In 1988 I was delighted to be asked to assist the National Museums & Galleries on Merseyside with the exhibition they were planning to mark the 150th anniversary of the race the next year. It was just fascinating, being attached to such a project and the three month long exhibition, which attracted over one million visitors to William Brown Streets Liverpool Museum, contained countless exhibits of trophies, oil paintings and even a life size model of Bechers Brook. Among those who lent valuable items were Her Majesty The Queen, The Queen Mother, Mr. Paul Mellon and the widow of a man I'd known so well Fred Rimell. Shortly before the 1990 race I was again put to use, this time building a typical Aintree fence for a National display at what had once been Exchange Station in the heart of the city. Now a very prestigious complex involving restaurants, offices and exhibition area and renamed Mercury Court, it provided a rather strange feeling constructing that National obstacle as I had so many times in the past, only this time seven miles from the racecourse.

Now as merely a spectator among the many thousands who each spring gather at Aintree, I enjoy the race without any of the anxieties I shared with so many wonderful colleagues for so many years; yet my thoughts each National day are with both past and present friends who helped make mine truly a labour of love. I watched in 1987 Jim Joel achieve his long-awaited triumph with Maori Venture; marvelled at the brilliance of Brendan Powell's recovery at Bechers with Rhyme N' Reason in 1988 to score a stunning victory and at a time when the National yet again became the subject of critical scrutiny, in 1989 cheered home Little Polveir.

The unthinkable happened in 1990 with major alterations being made to Bechers, but even so Mr. Frisk's win was as memorable as any which went before. And slap bang up to date, came that most recent epic race in 1991, when a stout hearted little New Zealand bred horse justifiably made the Grand National Seagram's. To see that, oh so young looking, jockey Nigel Hawke, persevering with such resolution on Seagram when Jenny Pitman's Garrison Savannah seemed certain to succeed, brought back memories I shall treasure forever.

There was a sequel to my recent excursion to Aintree and one which has provided much joy. As promised five years before, Vaclav Chaloupka came back in 1991, this time to ride the Czech mare Fraze. During his three weeks in Liverpool, we spent much time together and our friendship developed. Sadly in the race, Fraze was pulled up and when they departed the following day for that long overland journey back to Czechoslovakia, I could but hope it would not be too long before we met again.

I was invited with a companion to be the guests of Mr. Chaloupka and his family at the Czech Derby in June and again for their version of the Grand National at Pardubice in October. Words could never convey the incredible experience bestowed to us with such natural generosity of kindness on both our visits to Prague. To share such warm enthusiasm for all things equestrian, which the Czech people possess in such abundance, was refreshing in the extreme, making it impossible to believe that we were in a country which has suffered the domination of foreign powers for more than forty years.

Chaloupka's own racecourse at Tochovice is set among lovely rolling countryside, his administration block, stud and training headquarters housed in the nearby ancient chateau and the numerous race-meetings held there are a credit to his organisational ability and knowledge of the sport.

Visiting Pardubice was like travelling back in time to the early days of steeplechasing, except for the fact that here again efficiency and courtesy are priorities. The racecourse is a legacy from the days of the Austro-Hungarian Empire, winding as it does through the most beautiful baronial parkland and although at first glance it seems a confusing track, there are plenty of runners for every race and nobody gets lost. Vaclav, who carries the title 'Master of Sport' with commendable dignity and modesty, was attempting to win the 'big' race for the fifth time that

Left: The Czechoslovakian stallion Essex is cooled down in Paddock Yard after the 1986 race. He was the first runner from Czechoslovakia since Gyi Lovam 55 years earlier. Rare facts like these I obtain from my friend and co-author Reg Green's book *'A Race Apart'* - The History Of The Grand National. The Marlborough Bookshop & Sporting Gallery, who specialise in Grand National books and prints, always lists it in their catalogues as the most authoritative book on the race and I fully agree with them.

Right: Two of my heroes - another picture taken in 1986, Red Rum meets Essex's rider/trainer Vaclav Chaloupka.

Ossie an Aintree winner!

'Mr National' to hang up boots

by Roy David

AINTREE course foreman Ossie Dale, the man they call Mr National, after his 30 years at the track, is to retire.

Ossie who lives in Lydiate with his wife Joan has decided that after helping build countless of the awsome Grand National fences, it is time to call it a day—he is 66 tomorrow.

BBC NORTH WEST

oadcasting Corporation
adcasting House
7
oad
er M60 1SJ
061 236 8444 xt

April 2nd 1987

Ossie Dale Esq.
22, Oakhill Drive,
Lydiate.
Liverpool.
L31 2LF

Dear Ossie,

Many thanks for your excellent contribution to Russell Harty's Aintree programme.

NOW OSSIE REACHES THE POST

ANOTHER chapter in the great history of Aintree is about to close with the retirement of Stable Manager Ossie Dale.

Mr National's special day

The late John Hughes presents me with a badge for 'Outstanding Services to Aintree'; perhaps my most treasured possession. John Hughes' early death was a great loss to Aintree and the Grand National as well as being a personal one.

Above In my little private museum at home. I have made shields for all of the winning colours.

Right I have got a lovely selection
of Grand National prints, photographs, banners, posters, china etc., etc.!! and a beautiful early collection
of enamelled members badges.

GRAND
1893
HALL

year aboard Drak, a seven year old. Despite competing with an injured hand, our host rode a superb race, leaping the notorious Taxis fence in classic style and cutting out most of the running. Only in the closing stages was he caught by the already three times winner of the race Zeleznik, who stayed on determinedly for a record fourth success.

I return to Tochovice this spring to assist in the construction of three National type obstacles, including a replica of Bechers Brook, with a view to the better preparation of future Czechoslovakian challengers to Aintree.

AND ALL MADE POSSIBLE THANKS TO A PLACE CALLED AINTREE

A photo soon after Seagram Ltd had come to the rescue.

WEIGHING ROOM &
NSADDLING ENCLOSURE
UNSADDLING
THE
WINNER

Left: A happy trio an hour or so before racing started on Grand National Day 1991, Reg Green (bare headed), Lord Oaksey (hatted) and myself (with flat cap).

Right: Dick Francis signs books before the 1991 race. This picture was taken by Bryony Fuller who has written pictorial tributes to Fulke Walwyn and Tom Dreaper in the same series as this book and my publisher is behind Dick.

Perhaps the greatest horse not to win the Great Race since I first watched it from the public footpath in 1929, was Easter Hero that year. He was second under 12st 7lb having spread a plate; the race was won by Gregalach. Wyndburgh was perhaps the unluckiest in my time - second three times.

The best jockey never to win in my time must have been John Francome. Here he is on Rough and Tumble jumping the third last, to be second in 1980. The camera angle makes the fence look small, but the fences were not small in 1929, 1980 or for that matter 1991.

In the Autumn of 1991 I went for a wonderful holiday racing in Czechoslovakia - I saw lots of old friends whom I had met previously at Aintree including people from Russia and the United States.
I climb down into the ditch on the landing side of the Taxis fence. This is the equivalent of our Bechers in their Pardubice.

I exchange mementoes with Vaclav Nechice who is the Course Foreman for the Pardubice.

46
RED RUM
1st - 1973
- 1974
- 1977
2 - 1975
- 1976